CHA

CHASM

Someone Took My Mind for a Walk

ROBERT TURNER

JANUS PUBLISHING COMPANY
London, England

First published in Great Britain 1999
by Janus Publishing Company Limited,
Edinburgh House, 19 Nassau Street,
London W1N 7RE

www.januspublishing.co.uk

**A CIP catalogue record for this book
is available from the British Library.**

ISBN 1 85756 446 4

Phototypeset in 11.5 on 14 Goudy Old Style
by Keyboard Services, Luton, Beds

Cover design Creative Line

Printed and bound in Great Britain by
Athenaeum Press Ltd, Gateshead, Tyne & Wear

Iago: Look where he comes! Not poppy nor mandragora,
Nor all the drowsy syrups of the world,
Shall ever medicine thee to that sweet sleep
Which thou owedst yesterday.

(*Othello*, Act 3, Scene 3)

This little book is dedicated to David and Sharon for different but equally important reasons, of which only they will be aware.

Note

Chasm is, in its way, a book in which synaesthesia plays a large part.

# Acknowledgements

Amongst many people, I would like to thank The Prince of Wales for the great moral support he has been to myself over the difficult years.

I have to thank W. H. Smiths of Swindon for the gift of a word processor, without which the writing of this book would have been near to impossible. In particular, Mr Michael Edwards, who was the manager at their Bangor Branch and took it upon himself to put my difficulties to the managing director Mr Peter Bamford.

Also my sincere thanks to the total stranger whose identity I still do not know but who knew enough First Aid to deal with me when I collapsed in the library in Caernarfon. He stayed until the ambulance came and then vanished. I was unconscious at the time and so not up to making notes or noting names or addresses.

Finally, to Gaia Technologies, Bangor, their invaluable assistance when I was able to afford a PC together with all the bits and pieces.

Foreword

Every year many thousands of people suffer from brain damage. One type of brain damage is Transient Ischaemic Attacks (TIAs). TIAs occur when the blood flow to the brain temporarily stops, causing areas of the brain to die. No matter what the cause, recovery is often a painfully slow and frustrating process. *Chasm* represents one person's journey to recovery which I am sure many sufferers and carers will be able to relate to.

During recovery, the sufferer must piece together fragments of memories. Rather like trying to make a jigsaw with half the pieces missing: what is remembered does not form a coherent story. The self and the external world blur into one and sufferers are no longer sure where 'they', end and where, 'you', begin. Tasks learnt as a child must be relearnt, but this time as an adult.

As a researcher into the effects of neurosurgery and as a friend of Robert's, I thought I had understood what he had been through. However, *Chasm* gave me the opportunity to perceive the world as Robert perceived it, illusions and oddities and all. Thus you are rewarded with a unique insight into the physiotherapy of the brain, usually a silent and individual affair. However, just as Robert never lost his sense of humour, so you must keep yours; after all, humour is the greatest healer of all.

Sharon Swain
Institute of Psychiatry

Author's Prologue

At this late date it has been difficult to put together any kind of relevant picture of the confusions I went through when I know as an unremembered fact that I was confused and I also remember that throughout that period occasional flashes of what one could call *reality* intruded. In what follows you will find, I hope, all of it: the confusions, fears, doubts and brief pictures of the real world. I make no apologies for the difficulties reading this book may present but do ask you to keep at the forefront of your mind, *I lived it*. You may well be tempted to say after reading a page or two, 'whoever wrote this must be mad.' You would be right and it is that fact which validates it. It is a short book and anyone with sense will readily accept it could not be otherwise, even though it does span an eight-year period. But you see, time was squashed. I experienced no days, hours or minutes as you would know them and therefore cannot write about them. But it is *not* a hopeless book; far from it. There is hope all the way through to its positive completion. Please note I do not say *ending* because that would mean the damage had been repaired and, as we all know, that cannot be.

One final thing before I take you on my journey. You will either hate what you read or love it, but you will not be able to remain indifferent to it. If that seems a vast egoism, may I ask you to remember that a creative artist of any kind can never be a shrinking violet. And I believe that throughout the whole miasma there remained a small spark that was *me*, the ego. And to do it, I have had to break practically every rule in the book. This really is the last thing. You should find plenty to laugh at because even at my worst, I never quite lost my sense of humour.

Take a Mandrake Root

Take a Mandrake Root and
water it with sunflower seeds
And in the sunlight watch it
Wither whilst your daydreams
last.

Take a Mandrake Root and
sift it with the starlight
Of a summer eve before Hecate
Kisses the lustre from your lifeless
Eyes.

Take a Mandrake Root and
Dance an ancient melody
Old in the memory of man
Before such stones as now are
Placed.

And on the altar of the godhead
was a druid's gleam
a dream, a dream.
An age-old Tantulus in granite.
Rock rolled in the dark, dark,
belly of the earth.

Take a Mandrake Root and
sing a song, weave a melody,
Sew a newness on the backcloth
of your memory; just take a Mandrake
Root.

Take a Mandrake Root and
Heed not the voice that
screaming, whispers death into your empty
eyes; a sable pitch that the senses
feel.

Take a Mandrake Root and
heal the hurt that tenuous
From the soil in blackness bleeds
And screams at daylight's
pain.

Chapter One

It was Alpha and Omega, but let me not be sad, for all the new detergents state that stains 'shall be banished', as if they never were. But perhaps it was the smell of woodsmoke that brought it all back, like Proust's tea and cake crumbs. I had thought I had drowned it in the tears of its own blood, left it lying in pools on the dark pavements of night-hagged streets where neons winked obscene messages at one another. I had thought I had got over it; that it had left me in the ash, his ash, wind-scattered over the bridge in the harbour of his love. I thought I had got over it, physically, mentally and emotionally as well. Then there was the woodsmoke. Was it ironic and apt that it came from the burning of some old doors by some men demolishing a house? I had rolled past the site – or should that be sight? – on my way home. Home? A sort of mouse-trapped cupboard, shuddering in the winds of a bitter year, where I had tried to sleep away the tattered remnants of loneliness. This following the misted up daymare of eight other years, or was that hours? Minutes? Seconds?

Was he lonely I wondered? I doubted it. He had never been lonely. He always was. He, the one who was loved, cherished and now was lost. No, that was wrong. I was lost. Somewhere between Then and Now I had lost myself; had crossed some invisible barrier into another world. Well, maybe it was the same world but it looked, smelled and tasted different. I could not be sure it was real; whatever that may mean. I only knew that I was in it and that I did not like it very much. But it was Alpha and

Omega. And Tat Tvam Asi. That Art Thou. There were others to love beyond my blistered skin. My mind made a trade with the Darkpastplace-sometime-when and the Dream Scheme awoke as I had reached out beyond pain and through the Instant Minute of Eternity. This was how and I could not take it back to the shop and ask for my money back. There was No one in the Front Office and he's always an awkward bugger to deal with. But could I ride out this storm too or had I blown myself out? Puffed up like a toad in a futile, bleak defiance. Only needs a needle to destroy the effect. A key turned in a lock gratingly, like my ego against a reality it was unwilling to face.

Eight years of darknesses, doubts and confusions. To separate them out is like trying to part yoghurt from its culture; sticky, messy, difficult and utterly pointless. A bit like changing one's own opinion of oneself! Having got this far, beginning with death, are you willing to wander with me down a fractured memory lane of fear and fancy? One that winds from past to future or should that be the other way round? I don't know, and neither do you, if *you* are there, which of course is a matter for speculation if you believe Bishop Berkley. Me? Oh I'm with Eckhart, 'the more God is within, the more without.' At least I understood the latter easily enough, it was the former that took a bit of swallowing. But then one swallow never makes a summer does it? Isn't that a stupid statement? The one thing swallows make are nests! The one I'd made felt twiggy and uncomfortable. Stroke, a plural in fact, but strikes, not miners' ones or even minor, Jones or otherwise; and TIAs (look it up, I can't spell it). Did I make those or did they make me? Mixed with a black pudding of a sixteen-year-old's death. Alpha and Omega! Really! Oh Socrates, where is your, chariot? Where is your cave? Ah well, perhaps that is something I do know about. Autobiography. That's a thing a bit like a motor car except that you have little in the way of brakes and even less control. Life doesn't like smart arses. Anyway this is a bit of mine. Now look, you've started so you may as well continue. Which bit? Well you know when you're in a rowing boat and you miss a stroke (hello we're back to those again); it's called, 'catching a crab', is it not? Only there isn't a crab there. You've caught nothing. Well, that's the bit I'm going to tell you about. The Nothing. The whole eight years of it or, as I said earlier, was it only hours? It's not going to be easy, no one told me that. He gets in everywhere, like sand in your sandwiches or the puncture in a tyre that always happens when it's raining.

My world was a strange place where soft lights flickered a grey dawn into wakefulness. Shadows of people living their own protracted nightmares flitted across the cold vista of my vision, barely seen. Even in the quiet of my own room they appeared, as memories, happenings, events, all placed in a subjective time that refused to acknowledge the existence of reality. Why did they? What was their aim? Were they trying to drive me mad, or was it that they were mad themselves? Mad, searching for a kind of sanity that would let them live in peace. Free from the torment of not knowing. No one had anything to say about it so I turned over, or tried to, under the covers.

Half past four. School coming home, tired. Accident. Why? Car written off, but nothing, there was nothing. No reason why. Verdict. Reckless driving. Forty-pound fine. Only me hurt, No one wasn't there. He never is when he's wanted. But, that, that was when the dark began I think. Nor did the accident cause the darkness but that its rising caused the accident. The hospital was cat's paw quiet except for the bead's click of the nurse's heels on a floor so polished it glistened like the wistful sheen of lake water in a lonely valley. But what had happened? No one knew, but as already stated, he wasn't to be found anywhere. Naturally I searched my mind where it was laid out on the hospital bed. My body was there as well, of course, but I wasn't using it for the moment and had left it alone, as one does an unwanted supermarket trolley after unloading it. I felt a bit like Canute must have done when he requested that the tide stay where it was. Mind you all he got was wet feet. Me, I broke a bone in my neck. Doesn't seem fair does it? I mean there he was trying to tell Nature what to do. And *all* he gets is wet feet. Me, I get a broken neck just for trying to get home for my tea. Look, if this seems a bit confused, and I expect it does; just put yourself in my shoes; not Canute's, you'll get wet feet. On the other hand you'd better not put yourself in mine either, or you might get a broken neck.

It was a beautiful summer evening. Bright and clear, just a few cloudlets playing kiss in the ring with the sun. I remember leaving the main A5 and turning off to Llanberis but from there nothing. Someone, he's one of No one's relatives, took my mind a walk. Yes, know that's a quote but I can't remember whose. Did I fall asleep at the wheel? If so I drove for some five miles in that state as I had the accident less than a mile from my home. Hindsight suggests that it was a TIA, maybe the first of what were to become many and from which I still suffer. But my mind had flowed into a tumescent night and fingered the patches of colour that determined what I saw as daylight as on a fixed screen. A fairly simple injury, from which I did *not* recover as the medics thought I should; because for me the tide had gone out, and the white wrack of the spume pitted the sand into patterns incredible. My destiny awaited.

The TIAs unrecognised by us, multiplied aplenty, although I continued to teach for a while after treating the car to tea with a wall. And slowly the days, hours, minues were side-stepped and difficult to be registered, noted, as belonging to my life. They belonged to my wife, my children, my loves, my friends, to everyone. But to me they swept on blind and oblivious to the ruin left in their wake. Blind and uncaring. Blind and mindless.

This is real. That is to say it exists. But there is nothing else you can say about it. I mentioned Canute earlier and, of course, I know he was only trying to point out that *he* was merely a man. But that is the interesting point. Protoplasm, flesh, bone, chemical and electrical impulse, add them together and you've got a man. All right – human being. Homo sapiens, a being. What else can you say when you've said that. Well, you could say people. These were the shadows that surrounded the being known as I.

I, Ego, Id, Karma, Astral, Ka, Soul, Life Essence, The Not I, the Not Being. Man. Tags all, names, attempts to understand the incomprehensible. The answer does not lie in the name or a collection of names. It lies, lay, in the world of the individual. My world, your world, everyone's world. But my world had contracted like a black hole. And around me were the Shadows that should have been people had they coalesced into something more tangible; if they they had *understood* their *lack of understanding*.

The Shadows affected me though. They stopped me from being entirely alone. There was a sort of thread connecting me to them. They were humanity. I was humanity but whether they felt things as I did, I did not know. Likeness is *not* and cannot be the same *as*.

I wandered up from a memory and into a childhood wood where the autumn trees had goldened themselves into a last defiant glory before winter stepped in and destroyed them a little while. I found myself walking about and thinking. An odd occupation? I chuckled and spoke out loud to the wallpaper, clinging like a frightened child to the wall in the womblike darkness.

'Not really. All you have to do is activate the grey cells in your cranium and well – think.' It was not difficult, a bit like riding a bike. Until you have you can't, and when you have, you can't forget how to. The problem was that it was a bit like listening to 'Yesterday In Parliament', a Bach Cantata and a bad soap opera, all at the same time. And the leaves of the stray wood were noisy under my feet, so I set about watching the world through my own particular glasses, rose-coloured or otherwise. Reaching conclusions about the nature of existence. They were always the same as the ones I'd had the year before or even the minute before last; but they never ceased to be fascinating. They were not real conclusions at all. I admitted that to the draw sheet whose underneath crackled plastic platitudes. But like the Shadows in my room, I kidded myself they were. Pronouncements, all basically the same but each had its own nuance; each strove to spring from my lips, eager to spoken and then, and then, ah well ... They were thrown onto the scrapheap of yesterday's ideas. In fact they were yesterday's ideas, rehashed and as bloodless as a dying vampire.

Now there is an interesting conjecture! Not that vampires do exist, but why did people believe they did? Could it have been for the same reason that they believed in a god? A supernatural entity. I suppose vampires were supernatural entities; maybe are.

No one heard me laugh.

'I'm a vampire. Come up to my room and let me show you my etchings. I can say with absolute honesty that I have no intention of raping you.' Just think, an honest vampire.

'But *they* still need gods, whoever *they* are,' I speak out loud, pause and then continue.

'Come on, shadows. You must have opinions of your own or are they all formed by Murdoch? Oh do come on! I was only kidding when I said I was a vampire!'

Earlier in space I had met a man who used to be one of my lecturers in my youth. He had been Real. Perhaps that was it. The Shadows only became Real when they had some tangible effect on me as this man had done. But very little was tangible any more. And I wondered idly if my old friend had ever wanted a god. Could have found him one from somewhere. There's always the odd one lying about.

'Hurry, hurry, hurry, get your gods here, only ten quid a time!'

That was Riley, the god-seller. Used to be a fairground barker, vulgar fellow, I liked him.

'Hello, Riley, haven't seen you in ages. How's the god trade?'

'Oh middlin' fair, business ain't wot it used ter be though,' he frowns and pulls a grimy fag packet out of his pocket with an even grimier hand. Takes a fag out, lights it and chokes violently. Shaking his head, partly to clear it after inhaling the smoke and partly to indicate sorrow, he went on.

'The old god trade ain't wot it was. They just don't seem ter want them anymore.'

I mutter something sympathetic and asked why.

'Don't rightly know. Oh they've got their technocracy, but it don't replace the good old fashioned god. Leastways it don't in my eyes.'

I am not surprised as his eyes are bleared and blood-speckled yellow globs.

'There's still a few buys,' he went on, 'but it's mostly this modern rubbish made out of spiritual plastic. No bloody craftsmanship in the mass-produced gods those snotty little evangelists sell!

The days went by, or was it weeks? Either way, they went. I continued teaching and I think I did my job well; but then came a summer term which, for some reason I found extremely difficult to cope with. I seemed to be running on automatic pilot, except that the pilot had some sort of malfunction. The end of term arrived and I was, like all teachers at that period of time, tired. No, I was exhausted. And, instead of the usual pattern of going away after a week, the exhaustion stayed; glued to me, limpet-like. No, that's wrong. Leech-like, as it sucked, not my physical blood but my emotional resolve and left me a husk, a threshed seed of corn, bleached of colour and life.

We went to the doctor and after a few blood tests pernicious anaemia was diagnosed, which of course I still have. That complaint is similar to the relatives you can't stand. *Always* with you, you can't get rid of them. I never returned to the classroom, for by the beginning of the autumn term the Daymare had begun in earnest. What I had experienced previously was but a pale shadow of what followed. And I *must* ask you to keep that in mind; me? I am not sure if I had a mind to keep. Or if I did *it* was buried in depression, fear, confusion and doubt. There were small pools of lucidity, but they were rare and not altogether precious as you will discover. What's that? You want a happy ending? Well, doesn't *this* prove that you have one? Mithras has spoken from the tomb of Wledig. Ambrosius to those who do not know his Welsh name. If that connection seems a little tenuous, it should become clear and, yes, Riley does have a little to do with it. Remember friend, and if you are reading this *Other Naked Lunch*, then you *are* a friend. That I, and all the others on that list, have little memory, well what you would properly think of as memory. This is a reconstruction from a crudity, from an uncut stone. And, of course, there may not be a diamond there after all. That is a risk *you* will have to take; in fact have already taken. But some *will* understand and watch with horror the disintegration of a Soul and its slow pain-filled rebuilding. How does one describe the fury, the rage that eats the skin from the flesh and the flesh from the bones until the Soul is left naked to the stars' unremitting and ice-cold stare; at the frustration of not knowing *who* or *where you* are? Let me put it this way: self-pity oozes from every pore and sets, chitin hard, outside so that nothing can get through this 'beetled' skin to the person inside. From inside, one cannot see out. Vision is either misted or warped and I'm not talking about *Star Trek*. I had lost, at forty-five, to put it at its most simplistic, the ability to do the work I loved best, next to my family. Ahead of me stretched a sewer of darkness with the rats of hatred bleeding from its walls. But I could not tell anyone. I could not speak. Words were miasmic sounds and therefore meaningless. David, my friend, has asked me to try and tell it as it was. So far you have but tasted just a little from that bitter cup.

But reversing the usual laws; it is a bitter cup with a sweet aftertaste. I did not know, *could not*, the heartache and pain I was causing those who loved me and whom I loved.

Understand that whilst I existed during those eight years I do not remember them as you would normally think of them by the word. Yes, I saw people, doctors, specialists, nurses, counsellors and friends. I do not recall them clearly, they were spectral and sometimes very frightening. You will see things as I did or as near as I can get now; the pustule on my Soul having been lanced by, strangely, a third stroke and the death of Owen, my beloved son.

A delicate dichotomy. Moon-spun moments fled into the distance and on the horizon loomed a Torquemada with blood-shot yellow eyes. And beds were safer at night providing you did as you were told. Science or Faith. Faith or Science, why believe in either?

The angled path led straight up the mountain. Sundews caught flies like me in their sticky petals, feeding luxuriant under a malevolent sun. The grass let the sheep eat it uncomplainingly and soft rain watered them whilst they sprouted wool. My room was belly-pained and my mind ached. 'Oh when he falls down, leave him there, he'll get up when he's ready!' I did not know that clothes could speak. No one had told me that there ought to be a body inside them. I saw him and waved a hand in Riley's direction.

He, however, did not want to see me. 'Well, I must be off now, see you again sometime.' Riley vanished somewhere between the wardrobe and the chest of drawers with an evil smile. It used to rattle its handles at me in other darkness. The one when God switched off the sun to save on the electricity bill.

It was funny about this god thing. There were all those evangelists running around like some mad amoeba on a pool, all going in different directions and each claiming his/her way was the only right one. Oh, sure I know there are many paths up a mountain and one peak. But that is only all right if you are all climbing the same one. Riley, for instance. He didn't know where he was going but that didn't matter because he was only employed to sell the stuff. And anyway he suffered from cosmic halitosis.

The leaves under my feet crunched as I walked down the path. 'Meandered' might be a better word. I crossed over a little stone bridge, stroking and feeling its rough comforting surface with the palm of my hand. It scratched gently, roughing up my shin. Moss clung greenly to its stones decorating the blue/grey stone. Nature has good taste. There are some people on the far side of the bridge. I looked back at them in their blank standing coats of white. Their heart phones hung like dead fruit from their necks, each a medical crucifix only not even their earpieces could reach God.

There was a beautiful silver birch in the woods. It reached up to the sun in a fury of supplication. At least I think that's what it was doing. It had stood there for as long as I could remember, ever since I was a child. It was a living promise of life. A whole cycle could be witnessed by this tree. Birth, Growth, Decay, Death. But the tree is, in a sense, immortal; this because its seeds fell to the ground, were nurtured by dirt, took root in it and would grow into birches as beautiful as their sire. But the birch is a little like my Shadows. It isn't really silver, it only looks as if it is and then only from a distance. When you get up close, you can see its bark is pitted and scarred. When you are close enough the soft silver disappears and it becomes hard and cold. No one sat there looking very important and asking me questions I couldn't answer. At least I couldn't give him the answers he wanted. Perhaps I am wrong there and he *didn't* want any answers. But if so, why did he ask them? Whatever it was I said, I don't think it pleased him. Why should No one be cross because I couldn't give him answers. I didn't understand the questions. The seat was fairly comfortable though, but the room stuffy with disappointments. They leaked from the bland walls and were kept, when they were captured, in little brown folders. Sheets of shattered dreams and tears, line drawn, two dimensional and flattened until meaningless.

I became aware of someone at my side. I turned and saw a creature in an acorn hat.

'Here,' it said, 'take a leaf.' It held one out to me. I withdrew my hand but the creature persisted.

'Go on, be a devil, take one,' it smiled at me and warily I took the leaf.

'Feel it. Soft isn't it? See its veins, just like yours; its strength. Tender and fragile in the spring when it's young, brittle and easily broken in the autumn when it's old. Does it experience things like you do, or is it totally without feeling? It certainly doesn't appear to have a mind of its own. It just goes where the wind blows it and if you pull it off the tree it quickly dies. It never does anything of its own volition; just hangs about trying to look decorative, stupid thing. Oi! You! Don't drop off to sleep, this is for your benefit. Are you trying to look decorative? No, you're not good-looking enough for that. I think I prefer my leaf.' The small creature vanished, purpled itself out of existence. I scanned the bushes in the sound-splattered dayroom where I had wandered to after the doorway had been closed on the forest where, hidden in the caves and under the bark of the trees, the creature might have been hiding. The thing is I would have liked to talk to it but it hadn't seemed interested in what I wanted or needed.

Someone told me, tells me, that I had the guise of a strange normality (!?). A Halloween outfit is what they mean/meant I suppose. But what right have I to suppose they meant anything? Aggression, born of frustration, was boiling nicely on the Rayburn of the kitchen I had built into the converted barn that became our Doomsday home. I say that because that too is on record. The Rayburn isn't, of course, that came later, like the frustration and rage. That and the fear of the front door and No one who came, with his Shadows is a variety of fancy dress except that I did not fancy it.

What is kindness? A proposal to understand that which cannot be accepted as right and proper behaviour; to make allowances for, without judgement or the vain belief that one pattern is the same as any other. Ask anyone who knits, they'll tell you that the tension is never the same even if the stitches are. No one seemed to think that it/they should be the same as laid down by one of Riley's gods. One has to remember that Riley does *not* take quite so much care when he lays down his gods, as a wine grower does with his wine. Anyway this self, whatever it was, did not fit the standard pattern. No one even tried a special suit on me. It had quite a pretty pattern and like the most expensive costumes an expensive-sounding name: 'Progressive Dementia'. Sounds more like a plant to me, one that needs careful looking after in a gentle atmosphere. Anyway it didn't fit, the collar was too tight and the sleeves much too long. I kept tripping over them, they reached to the floor. Mind you, so did I, on several painful occasions.

In the morning when the dust had settled I woke up and surveyed my surroundings. My leaf had gone and so had my dreams. They had fallen to the quick death that precedes the rebirth of spring. I wondered if there would be any rebirth for me as all my Shadows were still there; marching alongside me like perpetual ghosts. No, they weren't ghosts, just vague impressions of a reality that my mind rejected; wished to reject because of its intangibility.

I wondered if perhaps it had something to do with the tea I had drunk in the company of my Shadows the night before. Certainly some of them had almost become real in the cold light of the Smarties from the trolley No one kept locked away behind a large rock in the dark part of the forest. But now, no, they were just Shadows; returned to their phantom shape and nature.

I knew they *could* awaken the desire to *know* in me but I did not desire the knowledge they proffered. Let them remain as Shadows. I went back to the beach. Back to the sand that knew me well. Every single grain was personal friend. I was accepted and known to be what I was. I watched the sea as it erased my footprints and knew that *this* was the essence of life. I knew, but was not yet ready to accept the finality of the thought. To not be, appalled the tiny intelligence that snuggled in the recesses of my mind. For I had lived the warp of my being and could accept nothing less.

Someone in the mist, bar-sparked day muttered, 'There's going to be a case conference on you.' How can you have a conference about a piece of luggage? On the other hand, that's what I was, a piece of luggage; a tatty piece. But if they were to have a conference on me, could I lie still enough? And where would No one put his coffee cup? I hoped it wouldn't be anywhere painful.

But then the dust settled and lay all over my land in a thick heavy pall. It knew no superior, acknowledged no master other than itself. The trees had changed and they too had become dull and grey, covered with the dust of a night's thought. Was this before the Smarties or after. Can't remember clearly but I know I thought of Riley and his god selling. I couldn't control myself, I laughed until my sides ached. Those poor helpless beings who bought his gods deluding themselves that they were purchasing a portion of actuality! Gold for a pig's ear! He's made a bank out of it, if not a silk purse. I looked out of window and saw that they had sprayed the grass. They did that every night to keep the dust of yesterday's stupidity from getting mixed up with today's.

'Today, today, today,' I screamed at the window and was sorry because it hadn't done anything to offend me.

'Good morning,' said a Shadow, 'would you like some milk?'

'No, thank you, just baconmilkeggcheeseandsomegoldinmy-teeth.'

'Come on, sit down. No one will be here to see you soon.' The words I had spoken were plastered on to his forehead but that was as far as they got. Too much learning in the way.

'Whichtodayistoday? Amondaydayorfridayday?'

He turned into a yellow plum, unripe, with a stone in the middle. I think he went away but then one could never be sure with Shadows. Someone wanted to dress me and a new bill came before Parliament as to whether it should be a blue shirt or a white one. In any case the tube in my groin had taken a dislike to me. Well, not me personally, I think but a bit of me and there was blood. It was blushing I think. The Shadow seemed upset and went to fetch No one. His caterpillared eyestalks and feelers did things but the tube would not stop blushing.

'Trauma,' said No one and went away in a white egg whisk. Well, you can't make omelettes without breaking principles. Someone held my hand and found a radioscope; it played music instead of heartbeats.

After the Smarties, the pain went on holiday to the Costa Del Llandudno. I hope it ate too many ice-creams and was sick! Why does No one not understand my words? My mouth is burbled and Graves's Claudius had filled it with stones.

I had to get well, *not just to get well*, but to *do* something even though I had no idea what it was. The Power of Positive Thinking/Emotion is not to be lightly dismissed. If I am not physically perfect, well, show me anyone who is. Not *admitting*, defeat Inside, when to everyone Outside it appeared to others I *had*, was/is hard to bear. Often and often, during the few and brief moments when I was at least partially aware. I longed to be able to shout. 'I'm here! It's me!' but I couldn't. The words came out twisted, warped and wrong, utterly, utterly wrong. In some cases the exact opposite of what I actually wanted to say.

That said, the process mentioned above could not begin until I had ceased to be absent for a majority of the time.

It has been said that a period of great stress can either tear a family apart or pull it closer together. I think that view is a bit simplistic, certainly as far as our family was concerned. It did a bit of both, in that there were times when my wife could barely put up with me; but at the same time was drawn to me by her love for me. Thank God she never gave up hope. I have now had time to talk with many other younger *victims* (and no we're not afraid of *that* word, it is others who have problems with it), and their carers, and I have discovered that very much the same things pertained to them. Of course, each individual's difficulties all depended upon the severity of the illness.

Chapter Two

The hills were brown this year. Last year they had been green but the artist had decided to change their hue. For what reason I could not say. Nor will I attempt to, but facts are facts. I stood on the top of one of them and stared out at the cardboard horizon. It was clear and sharp, as if a knife had been used to cleave them from blue paper that was the sky. It was cold. I shivered in the biting wind cutting through me, as if I were naked. For a long time I had nothing to say and that which came to me was not worth the repeating. No one was annoyed and insect-like rustled his papers. Some of them were blue, like the sky above the hills.

At my feet the bracken nestled, clung to the hillside determined not to fall off. Occasionally it did, of course. Then you could sense the plaster but not Paris and there was no Latin Quarter, except in the names on the Smartie bottles. *They* told us that it had died but I knew this was a lie. It had fallen off and could never return. Each night a little man full of years and rough cider came up the mountain to replant all the flowers and bracken that had fallen off whilst we weren't looking at it. As long you kept looking at it, it was all right. Avert your gaze and away it went.

The night before. What night? There was no night before as it seemed there would be no nights in the future; no tomorrow, no yesterday, only the blind unseeing today. Today I am alive but tomorrow I shall be dead. At least I shall not feel the bitter cold that is today. The cold, the cold, a freezing impersonality, a blank space in the nature of things. They were not aware that I knew and I hid my knowledge well. The padded cell with with the tight fingers of the strait-jacket did not appeal one bit. I was no Dinosaur Man and friend of Susan Baur.

I knew that there was this little man though because I had seen him. He came as silently as a dream, his arms full of fake ferns. The mental picture we like to call bracken, sundew, moss and heather. Quiet as a spider web-building, he spent the whole night planting and tilling the soil, 'Ground of All Being'. No, he is never satisfied for his mind's picture is perfect and he, the Ultimate Artist. But this year he had painted everything brown. It muddied reality and I knew not the anguish lying in bitter pools on the other side of a sometime front door. And when I discovered it, guilt dragoned its bleak scales before my sight. I did not know the hurt I was sowing, rampant weeds in a life-sculptured garden but neither did I know that love was stronger still.

But my Shadows were brown as well. He had painted their passive surfaces with his brown paint. He squinted at me through his pince-nez.

'Evening lunatic,' he called to me as I passed him on the way down from the summit the Gotama told us about. He, too, the little man I mean, is on his way home after a hard night's work. I ignore the facile call and he, unable to resist, calls again.

'Hello lunatic.'

'Why do you call me that?' I ask, more than a little puzzled. His grizzled face splits like a dried pea when he smiles.

'Well,' he mouths, cracked lips hardly able to form the words, 'you are one, ain't yer?'

I wax Socratic and inquire, 'That depends upon how you define madness.' I step towards him and he backs off quickly, almost disappearing into the chair.

'Now you keep away, do you hear?' There is a tiny ring of command in his voice and I know that if I touch him he will paint me out of his picture next year. I do not want to be no more just yet, so I grin foolishly.

'No old man. I am *not* mad. I just see the world as it is and not how you would have me believe it to be.'

'Aye,' he says, 'p'raps yer does. Well, I must be getting along I want me brekfust.' He turns to walk away and I call after him.

'Surely you mean supper?'

He gives me a queer look which I put in my pocket along with all the others the Shadows and No one have given me. Then he shrugged his shoulders, picked up the mountain and went off down the corridor.

He isn't a Shadow. There is something solid about him even if he is a bit thin. No, he's certainly no Shadow.

However the mountain is quiet now that he's gone. It belongs to me again and I'm not going to let anyone take it from me without a fight.

Across the valley, just out of sight, is the stone house of my home and heart. I cannot see it, but I can it feel it and *reach* out with my mind and soul. In it is *The Lady*, *She* who sometimes I think I know. From her there is a swell that feeds me, eases the pain, and sometimes chases away the dark. And I *long* to know her name, who she is. But I know She is a Lady; a tendril of memory, wet road summer-morning-fresh, cheese, plain or tasty, and a wreathing strand of silver in a rushing valley. Rain-wet hills breathing a brown-green smell when days clustered like moths round the ephemeral candlelight. The brisk, crisp, newly polished morning air and the chattering from the open doorway of the shop. A cream and candytufted bank beyond the gate and a castle almost in the back garden. I *should* know. Tears, the wet kind that varnish your face. Someone comes in from an outside but she hasn't brought any Smarties. Kneels, changes bottle or bag, or something. Wipes my face with a harsh tissue. Goes. Gone. I turn my eyes. The Past and Gone was tangled with the present and I couldn't sort them out.

My wife and I had met in South Wales and lived there for a while. It was a very happy time and nostalgia has enhanced its nascent beauty and the gentle generosity of its people. I am told that on several occasions I thought we were *still* living there. And in the back garden of the School House, my wife was the teacher, there were the remains of an old castle. Only the Keep, which in a way is very appropriate now. But, as in the north, there were in the south, countless woolly-backs, to keep us company. And in the darkness old memories were virtually all I had, as new ones slipped through my mind's fingers like the heavily greased pennies banks offer you and call them loans.

Across to my right there are sheep grazing. Chewing for eternity at a never-ending supply of grass. It doesn't matter how hard they try, they will never be able to eat their way through all of it. Fifty thousand sheep, each with a job to do. Always dressed in the same pure wool overcoats and all carrying the same vacant expressions on their faces. I wonder what goes on behind those unseeing eyes. I know they are shortsighted because they don't recognise me until I am on top of them. When they *do* see me, they all charge off in a million directions. I don't think they pursue any thought for long, as their minds are land-locked by their own stupidity. I suppose they have feelings but they are undetectable, too much fluff in the way. Someone is clicking in the corridor. Are they coming to see if *I* am here, or will sight of my body satisfy them? It does. Someone goes away again. At least, Someone does after a time has passed; after the hands of the clock have described part of a circle. And there was laughter. I think it was laughter. All right, a *noise*, but a pleasant one. And there was music, gentle music. Not from instruments but from voices. Someone was calling me. But I could not answer, there was too much fog and static. Well, this Someone was nice. A she? I don't know. Perhaps it was. I think I cried, but then I often did. They used my tears to make electricity and saved the government and the electric company millions.

I am at a loss this Saturday in July 94 to explain, to tell, what the thing that purported to be me, did during those eight years. I know now that I caused a great deal of worry and pain. That I was aggressive, at least verbally, but I do not remember. There will be those who say that I do not remember because I do not *want* to. I, or my wife, believe this to be the case because of the seed change that followed the third, my last, stroke. After it my personality was, how shall I put it, repaired, mended. I became as I had been before the first. Julia says that on many occasions something, not me, not the man she loved and married, looked out at her and, in tones that were ice cold, told her she was a nothing. This person now no longer exists and at this distance it is near impossible to believe it *ever was*. Of course, sometimes my speech was so slurred she could not understand a word I was saying. That *must* have been a blessing beyond measure. But you can see how guilt-hagged I feel now. And yet, I am told, there were also occasions when I seemed, 'normal', and by that I mean I apparently carried on a rational conversation. I say 'apparently' because I cannot remember these occasions either. But I *do* remember, very clearly, my sons Owen (whose death is at the beginning of this), and Andrew saying, some little while after my third dance with possible death, 'It's nice to have you back, Dad.' And though they both said it on separate occasions, their words were uttered in a way that suggested I had been away on a business trip. Well, maybe I had in a weird sort of way.

I am sighing as I type these words because I do not know how to put over the sorrow I feel for those last years. The other day my eldest son, Lawrence, made a comment about a problem he had experienced with an English teacher at school. I asked him why he had not come to me with it at the time. His reply was *devastating*. He looked across at me, where I was sitting in my wheelchair whittling away at a piece of wood and said, simply and *without any emotion*, 'You weren't very approachable at the time.'

I do not think I need to add anything to his words. Any of you who love their children will easily imagine how chilling they were. They, the children, except for Christopher who was only two when I became ill, have all said that they knew I loved them. That the creature they had to suffer was not me. Not the father who had told them stories when they went to bed and so on.

This reportage is the best I can do in trying to explain their reaction to me. They have made it clear, very clear, in their different ways, that they knew the monster that slept in the same bed as their mother was not their father. But they also knew and have made it equally clear, that I, me, the real father was still in there. He had just got lost, that's all. We live in the mountains and each one of us has experienced the mist, clouds, what you will, coming down and blotting out the landscape. And doing this to such an extent that everything becomes distorted. Rocks, which in sunlight are really quite inoffensive, rather pretty objects, take on a malevolence and threaten any and everyone who dares step near them. We do not need to go to Stonehenge to feel the majesty and mystery of Standing Stones. The Lords and Ladies we all know intimately. So, they could see *I* was lost. All they could *do* was to hope and pray that I would return. That and go on loving when commonsense said 'give up', and *love* they did, all of them. If you are looking for names, dates, times and places in this book, you will not find them. Indeed if you have got this far you will not require them and this little 'oasis' is merely to allow you time to take a breath before facing the desert again. For face it you must if you want to *feel* the clawed darkness that surrounded me, even when I went to the daycentre and was, apparently, 'normal'. I did wonder whether to call this a narrative but decided against it. So instead I think we should say it's a *natterive*, since what I am doing is, 'nattering'.

Even there, there were blind empty spaces, drawing my eyes away from the Shadows in what, I can only suppose, was a room.

I have just spoken with my wife and she tells me that all I would ever say about these therapy sessions was that they were 'closed'. By this she assumed I meant that they were as confidential as the confessional. Well, if they weren't then, they are now. I cannot remember any of them. All I see are as rolling massifs, straining away into impossible distances. The perspective is above criticism. Clumps of heather and scrub, making the picture complete; the texture of the colours are more real than they ought to be. I don't believe in you. You're not there. You're a fake. But at least I'll say this, you're a good one.

The mournful loneliness of my mountain cries out to me, to be comforted and loved. Yes, my darling mountain, I love you. Now don't cry, I said I loved you and always will. No one will not be able to stop me loving you. So just stay as you are, don't change and, above all, don't move, my faith isn't strong enough to put you back.

A long way off I can just about make out a dim coastline. That is, I can when the mist does not obscure my view. When I was a little boy I was brought up on to the mountain by an uncle. He told me that the thin blue line was the sea. It seemed impossible, so, a little while later I took a trip down there to see if he was telling the truth. He was. Just think mountain, all that water. Oh, I'm sorry, you can't think can you. You're just a huge mound of earth that can only cry when the wind brushes your sides. I wonder what my Shadows think of you? I've seen some of them up here but they don't bother me. They just drift across the scree, the tumbrilled scree, having daydreams of their own. I'm sorry, one must be politically correct, not daydreaming but indulging in autistic thinking. Anyway, I'm not part of their lives and they are nothing to do with me.

You've been here a long time haven't you, mountain? Always the same unseeing hulk, never changing, except to put on a new suit of clothes from time to time. But deep in that heart of yours you remain the same. I cannot remember a time when you weren't there/here, but then I'm only a couple of million years old.

Which reminds me. Did I ever tell you that I knew Socrates? I knew Gotama the Buddha as well. They weren't Shadows, neither was Jesus Christ. Did you know that, mountain? Oh yes, sorry, I was forgetting, Gotama knew each and everyone of Your Paths, Socrates knew about the Cave in your side and Jesus preached a Sermon from your crown. My! I bet there were a lot of Shadows around that day.

They came and went, went and came. It's like a never-ending stream. But then all streams are never ending and, in any case, you can never step into the same river twice. Logically speaking you cannot actually ever step in it once.

Permanence, foreverness, eternity. Something that never stops because it never started. Energy, pure and simple, never had a beginning because it has always been there or, if you prefer it. Here. Just like my mountain. As far as I am concerned you are immortal. One day I shall awake from this nightmare and the truth will either be better or worse than the dream.

That was the dream of my century. The black specks of life flickered and floated round my head. Antibodies attacking the core of my troubles. The substratum of my reasoning, the protective force that prevented me slipping into insanity. And kept me away from the pit of a tired hell that was so weary of its place in the corona of a warped time.

Mountain, you are my millennium. You were a piece of knotted string, the beginning at one knot, the end at the other. The placid self, unmovable. Your peak the old worn-out goal I shall never reach and wonder why I ever tried in the first place.

There is a sudden rage in my body caused by something I do not understand. It pulses through me, an ancient disease that I have come to know well. But I, me, I *hate* anger? Mountain, can you help rid my body of this crippling disease? No, I do not suppose you can, but thanks for the thought. God bless you, mountain. You are God-Blessed already, I know by whatever God happens to be believed in at the time, at any particular moment. And again some day has passed, or some month. It's all right climbing mountains; it's getting back down that causes problems.

Someone enters the field of my vision, the space of my awareness and tells me something. I *try* to make contact but its no use. Someone cannot hear me any better than No one does but they do *feel* kinder and I am comforted.

There is no doubt in my mind *now* that *certain* people did make me feel better, less vulnerable, less under attack and safer in their presence. I cannot say who they were/are, pick them out in some weird kind of identification parade, and maybe that's a clue. Their understanding and/or acceptance of me was far, far more important than who they were. In other words they put their own egos to one side for the period of time they spent with me. That I cannot remember exactly who they were would not, I think, bother them one little bit because they were acting from selfless motives and were not looking for any kind of kudos and there was a definite eirenlicon. A good example of this is the lady who was my first speech therapist. I have a blurred, out-of-focus picture of her in my mind, but just who she was has gone. No, that's wrong *she* has *not gone*, her warmth, her caring being has stayed with me. I know I was not *ever* going to be entered into her 'book of successes'. I would very much doubt if she, and others like her, would even dream of keeping a list of her successes. All I know is that it was patently clear that all she wanted to do was to help me get better. Her delight, pleasure, whatever, lay in how well *I* did, *not* whether she had been in any way instrumental in that success.

Chapter Three

In the cluttered house, under the dark corner of the stairs a mouse twitched in uncontainable fear. Psychic impressions clung to the walls like cobwebs as did the distinct smell that meant a kind of prison. Some of them were cobwebs, the cobwebs of thinking confused. Its empty rooms screamed a terrible silence that almost deafened the listener. Bared boards ached with the past and ached just as much for the uncertain future. And it was peopled with Shadows. My Shadows. I call them mine but I had nothing to do with their coming into existence. They were here before I *was* and will *be* after I am *not*.

Have you ever seen a place as empty as a dry well and yet as cluttered as a bad dream or a trip on the Tokyo underground? *This* is the house, where live all things imaginable and some that aren't. Such as a truly altruistic politician. What was it Shaw said to the lady at the dinner party, 'We've established what you are, all we're haggling about is the price.'

Here were dark things, black as the pit of night and as cold as absolute zero. Such are the nihilists who inhabit this place. They that know no peace and can seek for none. The erupted Karmas who will roam for ever and never find their Nirvanas. Here is an overlapping that cannot be sorted out into any form of logic. Although the Someones' each had their respective Mantras. They flow into one another. Sounds, voices, tones, sharp or dull, all without any directed cadences of any kind. There is a deadly music that hypnotises, fascinates and then kills them as dead as dead. And you can't be deader than that. And the Someones like my Shadows to play bowls, paint pictures or fix bits of wood to other bits of wood. And there were pale hymns as well as tuneless pictures. Fingermarks on the walls show where some one has tried to claw his way out. Blood and bits of skin show where his ego bled as he tried. My Shadows must have had a good laugh at that.

My skin is as rough unpolished metal and tastes of old oil. I dare not touch myself because if I do I know it will peel off in final lumps and stink. Then the Shadows will have claimed another victim. No! They will not get me.

Door. Wood, fitting a hole in the wall. In the door there is a smaller hole and it is called a keyhole. I do not have a key for it but I can at least kneel down and peep through it. All I had to fear was the Archangel Fear himself. And in this peeping, *you* are with me, as the onion skin is torn away. This, can I say confection? Perhaps not, serpentine creation then, is written for *all* those who *try* to care, but in particular for David and Sharon. The reasons why are very different but of equal value in a far from equal world and they will know them, for each in their own unique perspicuity drew me outward although they may not have known it. Though neither were present in throughout all of those eight years, *not* for *me* at any rate. But as we've found there cannot be a *Now* without there having been a *Then* and the opposite is true. Now where were we? Ah yes, the keyhole.

Outside I can see a new world. Well, the old one had to be scrapped sooner or later. There are bright streets. Walks of green and blue all shining with, as yet, an untainted finish. Everyone there is young with a youth that has wisdom. Pinnacles, towers, spires, tall and graceful, crowned the nascent horizon. Aerial machines move at incredible speeds across an evanescent sky. Underwalks and moving pavements, lights soft and ethereal and all created by a mind's ingenuity.

In my head a whisper of something someone I know starts.

Trying to tell me how to step outside and join them. A woman steps into my line of vision and beckons me with a grace no one has the right to possess. Her body is beyond the beautiful. Her breasts firm as she bares them to my soul. Without seeming to move, she is suddenly naked and walking towards me. I know that all I have to do is reach out and touch that soft and malleable flesh. The gentle curves of her thighs haunt my dreams a thousand years and I stand there unable to move either one way or the other, forwards or back. Her Mound of Venus becomes a cup of promised delight and her navel undulates, calling me. She spins on her heels before me allowing me to drink in all her delights, then:

'Come, my love, come; enter my body that we might be linked never to part.' Her legs part before me and I know I can no longer resist. But the key? I haven't got the key! I am locked in this room and cannot get out and kiss my love to a frenzy.

When I return to the keyhole the vision has gone; the world is no more. It has vanished and in its place is, nothing.

Have you ever tried to imagine nothing? It's like trying to imagine a food that has never existed and then describing its flavour to a man with no tastebuds. Whilst I am doing this, a sharp sound brings me back to my purpose. I am not yet sure what it is but my head peals with joy at finding I might have one.

The stairs of the old house curve upwards in a great sweep. The mouse still sits and shivers in its dark corner. Afraid of its own Shadow. That's curious; me realising that a mouse can have its own Shadow. I wonder if I've got one? I put *that* thought into the kitchen drawer along with the other bits of string, sellotape, screws, rusty nails, a broken comb and brush which has lost its bristles. Actually the brush never had any, *they* had been made of nylon. Anyway it doesn't matter. I want to tell you about the stairs and what lay at the top of them. I wish I could forget that woman, God she was beddable! I wonder? If I found a key upstairs and hurry back to the door with it, that possible future might exist for me? Like Schroedinger's Cat and the Uncertainty Principle. On second thoughts, I know it wouldn't because by moving away from that door I had altered the Present and, therefore, the Future.

There are a thousand bedrooms upstairs. Probably more than that, only I got tired of counting them a millennium ago. But every single one of them has seen birth and death. Loving and fighting.

My Shadows are so thick in the bedrooms I can hardly move for them. In fact if more of them had possessed form and function, I would have been as traffic-jammed as the M25. Thankfully only a few do possess solidity so I am not affected too much. I quite like my Shadows; most are vaguely friendly. Only a very small, only a very small number would hurt me if they could.

In the first room, a gold one with ornate drapes made of purest silk, are the principal Shadows of this world. But I know that all I have to do is bare my teeth and clap my hands and they'll disappear like water down a drain. Not that I would actually do it. But it might be fun if only to taste the confusion it would cause. Cherry pies are sweet with a slight but bitter aftertaste that lightens the palate and helps prepare it for more succulent dishes. That's why I like these particular Shadows. Like a good wine, rich in flavour and heady with promise. I have a large cellar of this. Bottles and bottles of it.

When I awake the following morning my head aches with the aftermath of the night's revels. Revels? Hah! How can you have revels all on your own? Sure my Shadows were there to keep me company but what good are they? They don't converse, only mutter platitudes into their beer and wine glasses. I knew nothing good would come of letting them into my wine cellar. They drank up, shut up, and left in alcoholic hazes. As they drank they became more Shadowy than ever. Drifting into almost nothing, never quite disappearing but becoming mere wisps of what they had been Before the drinking began.

Before the drinking began! I like that! Might use it some time, like, 'When the kissing had to stop', only Constantine has used that with great effectiveness. Anyway it might make a good title for the masterpiece I never intend to write. All the best literature has never been written. I mean who wants to rape a clean, white sheet of virginal paper merely to hear some obscure critic say it's a work of genius?

'To be frank, I do!'

'Get knotted!'

'You're an unprincipled bastard! Anybody ever tell you that?'

'Yeh. The bastard bit often. But ain't I just?'

'Stop bloody grinning. You're a greasy, unprincipled, speckled-bellied bastard!'

'Haven't you forgotten the "black enamelled bit"?'

Have you ever you seen your Self slam a door in your Own face? Most unnerving experience. There I stood on both sides of the door. One of me in a gigantic huff, the other vaguely amused.

I thought of other summer days when the sun slipped behind the clouds and only greyness presided over what had been light and life-full. Then I knew where I was going but now I had a heartache and a split personality. I have split and I am not sure that we, or do I mean I? – will ever be able to get together again. Each moment I used to savour, now even roses have lost their colour. Each minute of the finite day had its own treasure of joy. Simple all. You know, when you are on a train and wake up to find that you are nearer home than you thought. Now the journey seems never ending.

Dimly, in those upstairs rooms, I light my pipe and ponder upon these million happenings. Have they *really* only been a few short years? I know a thousand are supposed to be like an evening gone. I'd just like to know where they went.

My wheels take me down a long green and white striped corridor. Some strange tiger-like animal? My wheels don't tell me where we're going. Now don't be stupid; how could they? They're only made of rubber and have no mind of their own. And no, they don't rub marks out like other rubbers, they make them. And there are quiet sounds in the house. Rustlings, movements, creakings as the old place settles into its home-made grave. This house, the dome of antiquity, this sceptred—. Oh shut up. Just speak it as it was, a seemingly living thing in its own right.

What it has known it will not tell, for its lips are sealed. Its Soul's Windows stare out into the future. A future that could have been mine if I could only have opened that bloody door. That woman, oh my God, that woman! I *must* find that key, the KEY, THE KEY. I MUST FIND THE KEY. DAMN YOU! WHERE IS THAT BLOODY KEY? For God's sake, I must stop this. No – I – will – not – think – of – the – key – or – the – wo – mmm – aan. My two selves must coalesce again. I must be whole again.

If you walk, or roll, as you please or can, straight down the hall you will, providing you keep on walking long enough, arrive back where you started. You see this is a circular house constructed by a Master Builder. You can wander about for millions of years and never reach any particular place at any particular time. I know because I've done it. But don't do it, my child. Please don't do it! Children always ignore the advice of their parents. It's their prerogative. They have to find out for themselves. That's why this house keeps on expanding. Several millennia's children need an awful lot of room.

Now, collect yourself, dry your tears and face the next onslaught from whatever quarter it may come.

'Hello. So you've decided to come back then?'

'Yes.'

'Is that all you have to say?'

'Look. They lock people away for talking to themselves.'

'The Prime Minister's been doing that for centuries. So have we. Talking to ourself I mean. They haven't actually *locked* us away yet.'

'That doesn't prove we're not mad.'

'Well, if we are, so's everyone else. Anyway you shouldn't say mad, you should say endogenous depression.'

'Oh, belt up, and let's get on with the coalescing!'

'Okay, I suppose we ought.'

That's better, didn't like being two people at the same time; especially when they were both me.

What shall we, ooops sorry, I, do now? Upstairs. Yes, upstairs. How long have I been up here. No time. tIme.tiiiimmmeee. Stop that! Mustn't bugger about with time, my Shadows won't like it.

Hello Shadows, still there are you? You won't go away even if I tell you to. Nasty grey things, drifting about like obscene white corpuscles, ready to devour any innocent little bacteria minding their own business corrupting someone. The policemen of the system.

I knew a policeman once. He was all blue except where his body peeped out of his uniform. It was down on the main street of that town in the dimension I wandered into by accident the other week. Wandered? That's a laugh! Blundered is more like it; but I forget, you weren't with me were you? I daren't say that dreaded word again or I'll get a fit of the giggles and upset everybody for hours around. Phew, that was close!

Someone has appeared with a trolley. Reminds me of a fork-lift truck. Bath time. Eighteen undresses me and talks, I think. The water is too hot and then too cold. And the thing I dread more than having my bottom wiped, happens. My penis rises, thick, strong, and very male. But for the wrong person. Eighteen says nothing and for an instant I see bright, clear eyes, warm, friendly smile and an understanding. But then it is gone in wet flannel, soap and towels.

But you see, 'Now,' *that* is a precious moment. *Not* the stupid erection! The brief glimpse of the *real* that I can recall. The *smile of understanding.* A seaside postcard almost one might say. Such are the few moments, stills on the backcloth. No, I do not know Eighteen's name, or even if she was eighteen, chronology is of no importance whatsoever. Was she the woman whispered of earlier in this chapter? If you think that you're more stupid than I took you to be, and you can't *be* stupid or you wouldn't be reading this book. You will, by now, have fully come to terms with my uncertainty, not only with the writing but even with the thought of attempting it. What are the expectations of the one who suggested that I try? I do not know, but I doubt if it is this. And yet, I *must* try to draw you in and at the same time *make* you see that it was not a total. Well of Loneliness. So I am speaking directly to you. Yes, I hope that this book will be read by many, but each one is an individual and it is to you, that individual, I am talking.

The days of those years are mixed. I cannot segment or compartmentalise them. I cannot say, with any certainty, just where on a time scale, where we are now. As I said about Eighteen, chronology is of no importance. When I was very young my mother gave me a little book by Charles Essam Carter, entitled *Turn Again Shrew.* I still have that book and in it is a little poem that goes like this:

> There was a little bay tree
> That smelt very strong of bay,
> And if you didn't like it
> You could smell the other way!

It may seem hard, presumptive, egoistic, or any other epithet you care to use, but that is how I feel about this book. While we're recalling childhood, 'Are you sitting comfortably? Then I'll begin.' Again. Oh, and *do please* remember that my short-term memory is still far from sound. I am not complaining, just stating a fact. It is a considerable nuisance, but so is a cold in the head.

At least I am not like the Minute Man, whose brain was so damaged he literally could not remember anything for much longer than sixty seconds. A further difference between him and myself is that that he retained the ability to read and write. I did not. I had to relearn, beginning with the alphabet. Spelling remains a constant problem as does the mirror-writing. Looks all right to me and would have done to Leonardo Da Vinci, but is not a lot of use when one is trying to communicate something that seems a bit important. And of course communication is absolutely vital, which brings up one of the more hurtful aspects of what others *perceive* when they see someone having a TIA. For example, I watched this happen.

No one sees a woman weaving unsteadily across the grass. His little ears, speckled with 'it's disgusting dust', prick upwards. Unlike Mr Spock he isn't logical or Enterprising.

'Look at that drunken cow,' he mutters to his friends. I am sitting in a Soul-Dream near to his Conscience, so I give it a nudge.

'Hey, she isn't drunk, she's ill.'

His Conscience won't listen. It, like him, is only interested in what his eyes can see. He believes that the Sun goes round the Earth because that's what his eyes tell him. He probably believes the Earth is flat too; just like his head. My Shadows play billiards on his head, 'course its got holes at each corner where his brains leak out. They dribble down his shoulders and lapels like eggstains. Actually they are the tear stains of the woman who knows what he is thinking, because his attitude and body language shout louder than Concorde taking off. No one is laughing with his mates in the sunshine of their summer-day-drinking-yacht-club table by the river. The same one as mentioned by Heraclitus. She who was hurt, 'I felt I was a pariah but could say nothing because I knew my speech would only serve to convince No one more than ever.'

This is, among younger sufferers, one of the more emotionally damaging aspects of both TIAs and strokes. It is the total lack of understanding from Outsiders who do not know you at all or have only a passing knowledge. Your speech becomes slurred and/or one cannot walk in a straight line. Assuming you can walk at all. The assumption is that you are either drunk or a danger to them in some other way. It was not so long ago that this was brought home to me very forcibly. This was a person who I only knew slightly but had been in the vicinity when I had a TIA.

My wife happened to meet him in town while shopping. He asked how I was getting on, was I any better? She was pleased to be able to tell him that I wasn't too bad at all. Was still struggling to relearn how to read and write of course and still, unfortunately having TIAs regularly. His reaction took her breath away as it went something like this, 'If I was still taking drugs like that, I deserved all I got and my illness was self-inflicted!' I am not quite sure which was worse – his use of the word, 'still', with its implications that I had been in the habit of taking illegal drugs, or his ignorance of what a TIA actually was and could do. *And* all this took place about a year after I had been hospitalised with the biggest stroke, the last. For which he had known I had needed both physical and speech therapy afterwards. It took me several weeks to get over what he had said.

So, you see, communication is, as I said above, vital and you, the sufferer, cannot provide it. All you can do is wait for things to get better and, like most people, I am not very good at waiting. I always wait in a hurry. You can always tell when someone is waiting for something important because that is when they'll seem to be busy, busy, busy and jumping at every little noise. As a child I always thought that the Christmas and Easter Fasts actually meant that the great days would come quickly. It made a sort of sense to me then and in an odd sort of way still does now.

Chapter Four

I get/got so tired, so easily and want to know who I am. I asked Riley, the god-seller, if he knew, but he didn't. I remember coming down from the mountain and into the house. And I seem to remember times were there before that, but *now* I do not know who I am. It's no good asking my Shadows either because they never speak. At least they never speak sense. Mind you I am not sure that I do. No one never seems to understand, although sometimes Someone always does, just like Eighteen.

I think, therefore I am. I am, therefore I think. I think. We've been through all this before, dats de cart befoh de hors. All I seem to be doing is chasing my own tail. Well, would if I had one.

A monkey has a tail. A long one usually. He wraps it round the branches of trees to stop himself from falling off. It works, too. Aren't tails funny things? They stick out of your bottom like some backward-looking phallic symbol.

Did you know we get that word from the ancients? They used to put a mosaic of an erect penis over the doorways of their brothels. Why on earth they couldn't just write 'Brothel', I don't know. Perhaps the ladies of those times liked to walk by and enjoy the thought of such a massive organ like that inside them. On the other hand, maybe it was because they didn't like to write rude words on walls where anyone could see them. The only certain thing is that it proves that they had brothels. I don't think we're quite so honest now, in other ways apart from that.

For example, I saw Jack on my way here, coming back from wherever I had been to. You know, everyone's always all right except him. Anyway, like I say, I saw him but I made damn sure he didn't see me. Getting mixed up with him is as bad as coming into contact with his brother Jonah. What started him off was a slight problem with a whale. I seem to recollect being there in one of my incarnations. 'Course he was just a Shadow then, until some one decided that one of Riley's gods had a hand in it; that made all the difference.

Trees have a fatal fascination for tails. They just can't stop themselves from curling round them. It doesn't matter to whom they belong. The tree concerned always gets itself invited to the tail end of the party. And they kept mistletoe as a kind of pet. That's like a tail only with white lumps on it and druids thought it was magical. They used it to try and find out who they were. Just like the Standing Stones.

I once sat on a first edition of a stone and thought about all possible things. Unfortunately, my brain couldn't stand the pace and broke into tiny fragments at my feet. It took me thousands of years to sort it all out. Like a jigsaw puzzle only a little bit more important than a pussy cat looking over a farm gate. Oh, I don't know though. Jigsaws of pussy cats and farm gates have a specific purpose don't they?

The only problem with stone books is that the pages are a bit heavy, but Angel Dust, sprinkled from the stars' eyes both eases and causes the chemical miasma. No one told me that, well, some No one did before he vanished in a puff of blue smoke and a bad temper. He'd rented the latter from a Used Ethics Salesman on a short-term trial, just to see if it would be useful. Just after he left the Scribe came. Luckily there was an ink bottle within reach, so I could ask him to write down my experiences.

We left the inner circle of still-sitters and he wheeled me and my mind through the corridor and passed the museum. I looked in and saw 'She Who Was The Beautiful Heaulmiere', and 'The Caryatid Fallen Under Her Stone'. I thought Rodin was right but all my Shadows saw were the lumps of stone. From somewhere deep inside I remembered Heinlein's words on this issue. I wanted to tell the Scribe but he had stuffed up his ears with cotton wool and piped muzak. Heinlein said something like this: 'Anybody can see a pretty girl. An artist can look at a pretty girl and see the old woman she will become. A better artist can look at an old woman and see the pretty girl she used to be. A great artist can look at an old woman, portray her exactly as she is and force the viewer to see the pretty girl she used to be.' But the Shadows think the sculpture is just an ugly rock. Old Mary used to live in the village and I recall her as always seventeen, 'imprisoned by the ivory-sculptured years'. I hoped that, between us, the Scribe and I might find *me* somewhere among the molecular dust. M.A.O. Inhibitors notwithstanding or a Mickey Finn of Dopomine, your own or administered.

The Scribe, my biographer, was an old man with a face as brown as burnt chip. He had no teeth in his head and so he couldn't understand a word I said. He kept on getting all the sentences mixed up so I didn't know where I was. But we persevered and wrote our own *Pilgrim's Progress*. At last when it was finished we celebrated its completion with a glass of good beer, then we made a bonfire of it and kept ourselves warm for a minute or two. After that we went to the fair. You can never tell what you might find there; something different round every corner, always assuming you can find the corners to go round.

The fair was a wonderful place to be. All kinds of whirligigs spinning in a million directions. I like Carnies even though I knew that their job was to separate my Shadows from their money. We had a ride on the dodgems, trying to overturn all the little cars; it was cheap, only a thousand lifetimes a go. And there was the roll-a-penny too. My Shadows loved that, they spent hours there watching the coins, meant for Charon, roll down the specifically angled slot on to the plateau below. But it didn't seem to teach them anything. It's so nice to be without knowledge. Knowing can be painful. There was the bingo, computer games, fruit machines (I never got so much as an apple; Eve had it), roundabouts and rollercoasters; they were all there in gaudy confusion. It's the bright light that attracts moths.

I gorged myself on toffee apples and candyfloss until I felt quite sick. That way I knew I had dined well. My Shadows didn't eat much. At least I didn't see them eat anything. *And* there was the compulsory thick mud underfoot where the grass had obligingly turned itself into a mire. This made my feet cold after a short while, so we went in to see the bearded lady. My Scribe said it was a fraud because after he had tugged at the beard and she swore; he said she was no lady. Her beard was rather tatty too, just a few wisps of hair clinging to her chin like frightened children to their mother's breast. Eventually we became so bored we set fire to it. My Shadows ran. They ran so hard they almost became people.

After that we went to the river and watched some Shadows being hypnotised by fish into catching them. About six or seven hours they sat there and never moved once. Unless a fish grabbed their line and nudged them into some kind of wakefulness. Not being a good hypnotic subject, Someone tried once and went to sleep himself, I was not attracted to the sport. So I left the Scribe staring the water into submission and went.

And, went, went, went. Nowhere or maybe somewhere. Either way I knew when I arrived.

There was a tall, cigar-shaped spire of metal pointing at the sky. There was an artistic arrangement of struts all round it. I liked it very much, a shiny maypole, with metal ribbons. There were also some squat buildings not far away. Obviously tea and sandwich bars. You know I love maypoles but my Shadows seemed to get ever so upset when I knocked it over and it exploded. I was quite startled because never once before in my whole life had a maypole exploded. Now I suppose I shall have to find something else to play with.

Just then the Scribe came tottering over the hill so I hailed him.

'Hi there!'

He waved a feeble hand, perhaps watching the Shadows fishing had tired him out.

'Where shall we go Scribe?'

'Ai, what's that?'

'I said, "Where shall we go" you old fool.'

'Don't you call me an old fool! Old I may be, fool I ain't.'

'You're not as deaf as you make out either,' I muttered to myself but he heard that as well and brandished his ballpoint at me. He used it like a witch uses a wand except *he* wanted to turn me into a statistic not a toad. And he went on in a grumbly-rumbly voice, 'You mind your manners or you'll git no writin' out o' me!' Then he grimaced. You know the way old men grimace. They think they look threatening where they only succeed in looking ridiculous. I thought that he might tell me to go and paddle my own canoe, but he didn't, so I hired a speedboat and we went out for a spray.

While we were in the boat, the Scribe crooned an old song. It happened to be a mournful one. The sort of thing old men sing just before they go away. But when they sing anything at all they usually manage to make songs sound mournful even when they are happy ones. Such as, 'Let's Stick Your Soul on the Fire, the Price of Coal's Gone Up Again'. Anyway, this is what he sang:

The children of the damned
are dreamless in their sleep.
And on their brows lay heavy
furrows, from the witless waking
of the days.
I see their tender moments
Emasculated by their own desires.
Cloud-wrapt, in aching globes,
Stomach-pit-twisted where the
feelings hide.

There is no peace for these,
No softling moment, whose heart's ease
sings, blossoms, gives seeds and loves
in a silent commune.
Theirs is a time treachery,
De Sade, mindlessness and fear.
Who see only the cold blinking
of the stars, as purity on velvet.
Outreaching them, beyond their touch,
For they are down,
For they are down.
Wisdom, nothing in *their* hands.
Too short, and crumbling.

He had to sing it several times before he could get all the words right. That's why I remember it now. What's that? Was it moving? Oh, I don't know, I always use a purgative myself.

The river wound its way in ever-decreasing squares. Getting the boat round those corners was sheer hell. And all the time the Scribe just sat in the bows and sang to himself. I didn't really need him any more because we'd written one biography and I didn't feel like doing another. But he was company and I needed that.

The banks were crowded with Shadows. Many of them shouted to us as we went passed. But we didn't take any notice, we were too busy. Don't ask me what we doing because I haven't a clue. All I know is that the old man kept on singing. I felt like asking him but knew he would only tell me that it kept the crocodiles away. Which it did; somewhat disappointing really as it meant nothing interesting happened. Such as one of the Shadows falling in and getting eaten. And *they* would keep on shouting. Anyone would have thought that there was a boat race going on or something.

Now you mention it I seem to remember that there used to be races on this old river. I looked at the old man, you know the Scribe, for confirmation of this, but found he had died. I threw him in the water and went on my way; determined that whatever else I did, I would not wake up. At least if I did and it got too painful there was always the drawer with the lock on it. Code-named Lethe.(H.*ibid.*)

You see Panic gut-wrenches your clutch and crashes all your gears. It's no use anyone being cheerfully helpful and saying things like, 'Sort 'em out! They're all in the same box!' *You* can't *find* the bloody box. I am speaking of those moments when the chilling wind of realisation assaulted my Reason. When for a few minutes, perhaps an hour, I was fully aware of the world and my condition. A condition that might have been interesting to others and was indeed a pregnant pause in the confusion; to me it was terror personified. Far, far worse than little brown envelopes with seethrough windows. Worse even than a week-end with that revolting uncle we all have and wish we hadn't. Yes, there is an *intellectual* scansion but it's your *emotions* that have been buggered about with. May I illustrate friend? Thank you. I knew/know what follows. Indeed in those pauses, those photos, I may even have been able to call them to mind, but they were of little help even though correct. This is from the *Surangama Sutra*:

Sutra: If you wish to tranquillise your mind and restore its original purity, you must proceed as you would do if you were purifying a jar of muddy water. You must first let it stand, until the sediment settles at the bottom, when the water will become clear, which corresponds with the passions. Then you carefully strain off the pure water. When the mind becomes tranquillised and concentrated into a perfect unity, then all things will be seen, not in their separateness, but in their unity, wherein there is no place for the passions to enter, and which is in conformity with the mysterious and indestructible purity of Nirvana.

If you prefer something more Western:

Eckhart: This identity out of the One and with One is the source and fountainhead and breaking forth of glowing Love.

Okay, so you know all these things and others like them from the modern bibles of psychology or better still, commonsense. The point is that they don't help because all presume you are in a state of receptiveness, which you are not. At least I wasn't. The mud in the jar is The All. Sorry, you may not like that but that doesn't stop it being true. You wouldn't like it if a bus ran over your foot. But it would still be broken. And Superglue doesn't work on the mind. However, the mud did settle eventually but I did not really notice it happening, I was in no condition to and could do little to assist it. The body was still enough but the mind wasn't.

While we are on the subject, it will have come to your notice that I have, from time to time, spoken about God and god/gods. I do not want those terms to be confused with any particular religion or belief. It is important to remember that Solipsism and Pantheism when put together can prove anything. Further, there are many who think of themselves as essentially monotheists whereas in fact *if* they thought about it they would find they are not. Any student of the Bible, if they are honest, will readily admit there are many gods in it, all supposed to be just The One. It is very easy indeed, if you find that difficult, to show that there are, at the very least, two. The Old Testament one and that of the New Testament. And they couldn't be more different. The OT one is a vengeful, petty, vicious beast who demands we not only worship him but go in *deadly* fear of him He, it, I wouldn't bother to cross the road for. But Riley's made a good living out of him. The other, the NT one, as portrayed by Jesus (not that intellectual pillock Paul), is a forgiving, loving and merciful Creator whom one can trust implicitly. He makes no judgements and knows all our weaknesses and deficiencies. It was *that* God who held on to me, and of whom I was but vaguely aware, throughout that black period of attrition. He, apart from familial love of which I was served up great helpings, was the only Being who intruded into my Self and with whom I had any connection. Was there despair? Of course there was and not just for me. Pain too. Emotional for my family, physical and emotional for me. But *my* emotional pain was of an entirely different order to that of my loved ones. Mine was the product of confusion, lostness, not knowing. Their's was *by far* the *greater* because I was, at times, hateful and they, helpless to do anything about it. Knowing, as they did, that I did not mean it, couldn't help it and/or did not know I was doing it. Plus any other explanations or excuses, choose for yourself which ones you are most happy with; either way they did not make it any the less painful. Anyway you can see why I thank God for God – Muslim, Jewish, Christian or otherwise. Of course, I realise that I will have offended theologians of all shades; some because they believe in God but most because they don't.

I've only put this brief explanation down in order to try and clarify my God-bothering meanderings. It may be that you would like more but if I indulged you, and myself, I would instantly lose sight of the tenuous, filmy, insubstantial thing I am desperately trying to show. Here I am close to using the word, 'thing', in its Old Norse sense. But, finally, to put said cat among said pigeons: Jesus said that God is in all of us. Well, He would *have* to be if He is Omniscient and Omnipresent. That means, folks, are you ready? It means, *you* are God. So am I, so is everybody. Yeh! Shook me when the penny finally dropped. Don't worry, I know they crucified Jesus for saying it but they can't do that to everyone, including themselves. Now where was I? Oh yes, going mad, but not necessarily quietly.

I suppose it might be argued that my Brain Stem Net was not working properly, that is the 'generality' of the world was, taken in, as it were. But the Net's subordinates were ignoring the details. And, boy, did they make a good job of ignoring. I mean, how would you feel if you looked at a rose and it turned into the hideous green, monstrous head of an aphid, slobbering a thick, white froth? You don't have to be on some drug or other to see things like that. Hell, who would want to? But take heed, dear friend, for by now you are just that, never, never, never tell No one what you have seen. If you do No one will want to put it in a cage and label it, even if it is the wrong cage, label and all. What is it they say? All shipshape and Bristol Fashion. Fine, but what if you aren't at sea, except in the figurative sense?

Of course, being at sea even in the figurative sense can make you feel a bit seasick and dizzy. I had suffered from bouts of extreme dizziness and, such is the nature of the Beast, I still do. This dizziness, which looking back (isn't hindsight a wonderful thing, a back-to-front periscope), when I first presented with them in my mid-thirties, they were diagnosed as Ménière's Disease. A perfectly reasonable diagnosis, but I did not go on to the further development of the disease. These symptoms are tinnitus and a gradually increasing deafness. TIAs also make you very dizzy and this little example goes to show how problematic to diagnose TIAs are. And many people who have this terrible illness, Ménière's, have also been attacked by those who do not understand in the same way as myself and others.

The fear of being misunderstood, appearing foolish, stupid and the ever-present fear of unwittingly offending people, rides your back like a vicious black bat. Its claws cannot be seen by others but I can feel them, icy and cold at my neck. Consequently I could only take one of several courses of action:

1. Don't go out at all. 2. If you have to, over-compensate by being too loud, too outwardly confident, belying the fear clutching at your belly. 3. Be frantically sensitive and take the most innocuous remarks as personal insult. I have been guilty of each at different times, much to the embarrassment of my family. Knowing that you are going to do this does not help one iota. *You* are not in control, *the demon is*. And I do not think that is too strong a concept to apply. In fact, it may not be strong enough.

You are *always* aware that if you do happen to do something a bit odd which in, how shall I put it? – Normal People, might cause a laugh, you know it is going to be actively judged and usually you, the patient, will not be given the benefit of the doubt. But stand, or in my case sit, condemned. It cannot be stressed strongly enough how much this hurts. In fairness I must say I do not believe that people do this on purpose, they just don't think before they open their mouths.

So, out of a sense of self-preservation, you try to avoid putting yourself in the position where the above might happen. You try not to go out for a meal in restaurant, just in case you knock a glass over or put up with semi-covert glances of pity when your carer cuts up the food for you. I have been in situations when I have overheard remarks from other customers to the effect that, 'she shouldn't bring him out if he's like that'. The 'she', being my wife. I have also been told that I have tied my wife to the house. One person even tried to tell me, 'Julia needs time on her own.' *Who knows that better than I?* I submit that no one does. Furthermore, to refer back to an earlier part of this chapter, those who make such remarks do not know how much time for herself she does actually get. And I shall not deign to tell them. It they wish to believe that I condemn her to colourless existence I can only pity them their lack of open-mindedness and lack of Christian Charity. They are the victims of the Old Testament God. I know that here I speak for many disabled people, not just stroke victims. Education, it is said, is the answer. Indeed it is, but there are many who do not have the desire to learn. Ostriches have more sense than they do, particularly when the birds have buried their heads in the sand. But enough of this. Why should we bother with the waterfleas that skate about in the murk of their own mud pools. Having said that, Jesus and God love even the waterfleas as well human kind that bite you and leave itchy lumps on your heart. Don't try to scratch them, you'll only make your soul bleed. Now stop being so serious, Robert. You're supposed to be making people laugh.

Chapter Five

The toing and froing to the hospital, doctors, the daycentre and therapists (almost stereotypical behaviour) was, I am told, frequent and considerable. A crazy swings-and-roundabouts affair, through which but faint pictures appear. I do remember certain things and yet there is a cruel twist even to that. I will try to show you. Eighteen months, I think (see what I mean), before the last stroke, my mother died. Apparently I dealt with all the funeral arrangements in a manner consistent with someone in full control of his faculties. I now remember the death but not making the arrangements. Worse, apparently, a few months later, I had totally forgotten that she had died and my wife tells me I spent hours looking for her. On one occasion, at a time when I could still walk a little with a stick, I vanished from the house. My absence was not noticed for quite some time, an hour I'm told, because I had not taken a coat or, more importantly, my cap. The cap was/is something I dislike going without. My wife then came to my bedroom to see if I would like a cup of tea and discovered I was not there. My son Lawrence was sent to look for me. It was pouring with rain by this time and she realised I had gone out in just shirt, trousers and slippers. Lawrence says that I been waiting for my mother to get off the bus from town. It was difficult to convince me that we had buried her, not even being taken to her grave did it. Now for the *real* twist in this. I now *cannot* remember forgetting her death. Or that I went looking for her. The latter is probably more understandable than the former.

However, her death is now what I can only call a plastercast memory. I know of it, that is all. The anguish that causes needs no explaining. The other point is that this took place during a period when I had been discharged by one consultant and my GPs were trying to arrange for me to see another. They really had a struggle on their hands but never gave up with me nor do I believe they ever considered doing so. As I said in Chapter Four, I didn't fit into the usual pattern, any pattern as far as I can see. What did the King say in *The King and I*? 'It's a puzzlement.' And for me, as you can see, the real light had gone out of my life.

There was only a cold light in the sky. A blue, cold light. Cold lights are always blue, it's their nature. Like fallen angels are always burning. Have to, there's nothing else for them to do on that everlasting lake. A galaxy of the super nature and I have enough trouble with ordinary ones.

I don't know what to do about this Milky Way. It's so crowded there's hardly enough room for a body to breathe. I suppose I could unmake it if I wanted to by not looking at it. But if I did that some one would be bound to cry. But I must try to get back to my point. Cold is blue. It is, it really is. It has the quality of blueness. Can you extract it? No, but that doesn't stop it possessing the quality.

My Shadows are not blue. They are grey, having a quality of greyness. Not worthy of capital letters.

I am shivering. Ergo, I am suffering. If I am Suffering, then I am not it. It is impossible to be Suffering and me at one time. But I am me aren't I? If I am me then I am not Suffering. I suppose that's what the Christian Scientists mean.

Anyway, I am shivering in the cold blue light of the sky. It drips down in a slimy sheet of icy blueness which grips my heart and tries to *squeeze* it out of existence. Little droplets coagulating at my feet and round my wheels. They jellify but never become solid. In fact, they quiver, palsied, frightened of themselves and repugnant to all my senses.

The Catcher comes along the corridor chasing these little blue pools with his yellow stick. When be pricks them they vaporise, become a nothing.

'Hello you,' he says pleasantly. I like him. He is a nice man full of good cheer and ginger cake. He is a Purpose with a man to guide it. Smiling, I answer him.

'It is a nice day for a stroll.' He is etched against the skylight. And he nods his head meaningfully, pursing his lips he continues.

'Yes. And I'm glad to see that you're not creeping about that damp house of yours.' He squints at me from underneath eyebrows as thick as the Black Forest, without the gâteau.

'I've seen you somewhere before.' His voice makes it a question. I shrug my shoulders and say,

'Well, I've been around for a while,' and then add quickly as he frowns, 'not as long as you maybe, but quite some time.' I feel defensive.

'Ah!' he agrees, 'there's not many as have been around as long as I have.'

'You still got the Tree with the Golden Apples?' I inquire, trying to be friendly. An absentminded mist glazes his eyes and he nods his head vaguely.

'Yes,' he says at last, 'I've got it somewhere but at the present I couldn't tell you.'

Sometimes I can manage to look very mysterious. It's a trick I learned from Riley to confuse people when I don't really know what I'm talking about. Grinning to myself, I try it out on the Catcher.

'I, er, think I might know where it is if you want it for some reason.'

He merely chuckles and puts a fatherly hand on my shoulder.

'Oh no! I don't want it! There's no reason in looking for it. If I can't find it when I do want it, it means it doesn't want to be found.'

This complacent remark makes me irritable.

'There's not much point in having it at all then!' I sound and am petulant. Like a politician who's just lost a safe seat in a by-election. I can't feel sorry for *them*, they should have their seats screwed down, then they wouldn't lose them. However, I like the Catcher even if he can be infuriating sometimes. Clenching my teeth I ask if he can do anything about the Blue Coldness around my heart. Of course I now know about Virtual Reality, his was Virtual Unreality.

'Do you want it removed?'

'Don't be stupid, of course I want it removed. I wouldn't have asked otherwise.' He looks at me down the end of his stethoscope; that's a thing like a periscope only for seeing secrets.

'Son, I am incapable of stupidity. They left that part out of me when I was constructed.' He gazes earnestly into my face. I wish he wouldn't, it's very disconcerting. When people do that it makes me want to believe them. Ahead of us the corridor narrowed, and behind us too, slamming its mindless door; enclosing the world. Then, quite suddenly a smell doffed its cap at me and, recognising it, I felt a surge of desire. After opening the cell door we went in.

'Coffee please.'

'Yes, love, sit down and I'll bring it yer,' said a smile. It was a *she* smile and *that* made it different from the rest. But it died, almost before it had been born, by lips that were tight with inner terror and stifled all their children; drunk on infanticide.

I peered at the cell's interior. A calendar with dates marred by thick black pencil. A vague steam exuded from the shiny bulk of a coffee machine on the flattened abacus, one without beads. In the steel surface I could see the punctured image of my face.

'D'yer want sugar love?' a *tired hell* voiced from the well of its own isolation. I nodded. The wallpaper was blushed with nicotine and my mind felt as stained. The sudden silk in the warp of my life had a flaw and my fingers were too damaged to pick up the threads. Had we passed some plane trees on the way to this place or was that a mumbling memory of some other time? The circle that has no end was shattered.

'Yer've let yer coffee git cold, luv. Shall us heat it up fer yer?' She had brought the smile with her, dug it out of the drawer behind the counter. Then the cup floated back, steaming gently. I was glad she couldn't see the Catcher. I didn't want to explain him. It's difficult to begin when you don't know where you finished last time.

The Catcher took me out into the street. The Shadows were all over the place. Coming back from church, processing the path down to their graves. Coming, going, becoming, being, ising – all the same thing? I watched them, coffee slopping about in my stomach making me feel sick. Gate, wall, hedge, gate, wall, hedge, lamppost, wall, wall, gate, hedge, gate, gate. A Shadow passed. Female I thought. She didn't smell very holy. She went passed a lamppost and through one of the gates into a house; to swear at her husband and scold her children. Why didn't she smell holy? She should have done, but all she seemed to be was a bundle of perfumed underwear and fury, covering *starched* breasts gone hard in the bleak desert of her marriage. Dead hair peeped from under her hat; it hadn't even got the energy to fall out. It was scared of the sunlight. What ever happened to the woman-smell of love? It was the blue coldness I knew and I told the Catcher I had seen enough of *this* cinema and wasn't there another somewhere else? They might be showing *Star Trek*. I liked that, we both had impulse engines and warp drives. I wish the Catcher could extract the blue cold like a dentist does a tooth.'

Churches. The buildings I mean, always drew me during this period particularly the old ones and even more particularly when empty. Chapels too. Again I cannot remember too clearly but there was something about the way the ancient floorboards sang their history and the years of knees that had knelt on them. Then there is that distinctive smell of the hymn and prayer books, lining the back of the first pew as you enter the place. They are not merely dusty and hold, between their covers, not just hymns but the hopes, prayers, agonies and praises of countless unseen souls. Those and the memories of those who ever held them. In others it was the incense that drew me into the heart of the place, as it rose invisible in the silent emptiness to the God I knew was holding me as tightly as any of those past-people who might have held the books.

But I did not like churches when they were full and still have trouble with that, especially if there is a service going on. Again I think this is a symptom of my fear of people en masse. In small groups I am not too bad but in large ones I do not function very well. *Terror* clings to the fringes of my being and I am always scared something might go wrong. I might get my words jumbled if I have to speak or start feeling ill in any of the numerous ways brain-damaged people can. You feel so stupid and silly when it happens. It doesn't matter how often you are told it doesn't matter, that people will understand; because it only takes one to react badly towards you and bang goes all the self-confidence you and your loved ones have carefully nurtured over what might have been a period of years. Such is the fragile flower of your essence and being. You are back to square one and have start all over again. There have been times when I was so terrified of the Outside world that I would not go to the front door or even, willingly, answer the telephone. Many will recognise this as a symptom of severe clinical depression which is very common amongst stroke victims and, I suspect, others with brain damage for whatever reason.

Between the hours of wakefulness and sleep there is the blandness, possessing nothing. Empty as a dry bone, except perhaps its DNA and the Double-Helix of confusion. Just an empty shell of place-value that actually has no value, for everything is without flavour. From Nothing come all Somethings but all plausible features were veiled in mist, but a mist that was malleable because, if I knew how, I could mould them a million times a million. Most lie on the nursery floor, forgotten like the faeries. The Catcher kept trying to tell me that the Blue Coldness was my creation.

'Why do you torture yourself?'

The question perplexes me, for why should I cause myself pain, mental or otherwise? That is not rational. But the Catcher has asked and therefore must be answered.

'I do not!' This a shouted sound in a globe of absolute silence. There are no absolutes they tell me, but I know there are, for I have seen and felt them. Out there, beyond, far beyond the pain of the individual. Out where the stars are scattered thinly and the spheres of existence know nothing of *homo sapiens*. Where he is just one of many among the few.

The Catcher exuded a gentle heat and repeated his questions. My answer is a turmoil of words with less meaning than their sound. Try as I might I couldn't cloak those sounds with meaning. They were brittle with a Humpty-Dumpty quality. I cannot order them or rank them into some form that would lead to a meaning and the truth. They will not behave but run about like naughty children, becoming slippery in my grasp, at least the short ones do, like god, truth, justice, value, help and please. Longer ones were better behaved. They sometimes stayed where I put them until some Shadow came along with a vacuum cleaner, borrowed from the Civil Service; because they were thought to be untidy and had to be filed. When No one brought them out to show them later, something had been done to them. They had changed shape, been twisted and I didn't like their taste any more. Apart from that the government had said that they had to put VAT on the meaning of words. But I still cannot ignore what the Catcher is trying to say. I cannot ignore the depth of his speakings. And he waited momentously, silently and, I think, amusedly. He could not help me until I knew what I wanted, but he kept his net of abstracts at the ready. Just to try and catch my reasons that floated about like seagulls above a cliff, shitting on everything, but at least it was white. Collect enough of it and you can grow rhubarb. Trouble is, I hate rhubarb! Probably that's because it's like me; it can't make up its mind whether to be sweet or sour and ends up being neither. And the Shadows, probably No one too, keeps it in the dark all the time; usually by putting a bucket over its head. And my soul has oxygen starvation but it's no use cursing Riley, he's not even part of Front Office.

While we are waiting, the Catcher and I, the world folds in on itself; like the Anything Box Pandora had problems with. I hear no sound, detect no movement, the bushes, ward-seen from window bars, are spikey in winter's grip and stare silently back at me. My coat is thin in the wind which has a bitter taste.

A naked man, the Shadows have not seen, high on a bracken-covered mound of mud, watches me as I come across the field. He says nothing, makes no sign, hardly becomes. *He* is Now, always, for eternity, forwards and backwards, watching. Without eyes or ears. Has he been drinking methylated spirit I wonder? If he had not, how could he stand naked in the cold blast of reality and the Shadows' hatred of the truth?

No bird uttered. No dog barked. No kitten mewed. No frog croaked. No water rippled. And the earth under my feet clung, desperately trying to root me. To keep me in the one place. But there is no one place, just an everywhere. The land was black and darkling, no inner seeping from the cracks in the earth. I sneaked a glance at the Naked Watcher and knew him to Be. Being, ising, not where-ing or when-ing, but Nowing. He watched and kept strict count of the days until his final Knowing. A knowing that would break when Reason awoke from its long sleep. Until then there is a Winter Land, out of temporal time, as galling as soured wine. The Watcher had no children and could father none. He *was* the Watcher with whom I could not converse.

Below the instant of this happening I caught glimpses of the laughter from the dream world. Below this barren place was a fading patchwork of hope, without sense, out of context. It nearly but not quite met and mingled with this winter world but the Watcher's cold kiss drove it back into itself, afraid. I stood in Nothing's Centre at the echo of his being and then eased my Self into the next furrow. There I could see tears on his frozen cheek. For time unaccounted He had cried. Never changing, could not change. For a million years I had moved towards him with outstretched hand, yet not gained an inch. My progress was measured in thousandths, whilst He just had to Be. Longing to love but always unloved, hated even. And my Shadows held the cord which prevented me reaching Him. How I hate my Shadows!

Someone holds a mirror before my eyes but I cannot see myself. Only a dull image that lies. The moon in a pool of water is shattered by a boy's pebble but the real moon remains. So it is with me in the mirror image. It is not the Not I that I see, but the I. The Watcher casts no shadow, has no mirror image, but is real, ultimate, without question, if asking many. Here in the Outer Court the blue coldness is at its most intense and the air is barely breathable. My lungs rasp, my chest aches, strains with the effort of living. The Watcher knows my effort but cannot help for, until He is recognised, He remains a negative. The Catcher touches my attention and we go.

Street. Any street, wet with rain or dry with the sun's heat. There, there are my Shadows: milling bacteria in the bloodstream of the city. Sometimes they merge into one another and become impossible to see as separate entities.

Red from a screaming neon drips from the bleeding brow of an innocent building, beheaded by advertising. My Shadows drift by unheeding of the building's dying gasp. But I can hear its thin, high-pitched wail of agony, above their audible range or notice. The Catcher tries to take my hand, maybe does, but I cannot feel. I thought I would feel easier when the Watcher had departed. But his unseen eyes scorch my back with the searing heat of white-hot liquid gold. I look at my Shadows and see that they feel nothing of the Watcher's gaze. For an instant I long to become one of them.

When does a Vision cease to be an Illusion or does one need to wear von Helmholtz's glasses to show that what the eyes sees, is not what the mind knows? Like a baby's visual cliff or the, expect contact, that never happens. An E-wave pattern without frontal lobe damage but which intrudes upon my mind and makes butterflies from the after images of unsynchronised light diffused by contracted memory. My left, divorced from right, in the cerebral miasma of chemical dysfunction; a molecular Chernobyl.

Interestingly I met a fellow victim who said that sense of separateness, of, in his case, his left side, was so great he went into a psychological state of denial that it existed at all. It had taken considerable therapy before he could be brought to believe that he still possessed a left hand, arm, or leg. He was convinced that somehow it had been sawn off or destroyed in some way. He now realises that he just could not accept that at his age, he was in his early thirties, that he could have a stroke at all. I, too, at times apparently tried to deny that anything was wrong with me. I was unwilling to acknowledge the fact of my illness, a circumstance that added to the aggression I exhibited towards others.

When does Nemo become Omen? Things, all things, proceed by given procedures and rituals, from a man shaving or filling his pipe, to the celebrant at Mass. Maths consists of making statements about what is thought to be a static reality. (I know a few divergent thinkers would disagree with that, and rightly.) But I had no dynamic to my reality. Does that make it Vision, Illusion or something else? I did not fit the stereotyped rituals of life and was, therefore, beyond the pale in cross communication. What is it Wogan says? 'When God closes a door, He shuts the window too?'

In the deep backwoods of my mind there is a grim war. It never ceases because it had no beginning and will have no end. There are twin sorrows lingering beneath the surface of the desert; each dying because the other is dead already. In leaf-soft steps they tread across the sleeping embolism, not daring to breathe. A half-fear, unrequited and lost. Where is their value? Judgement days are never forthcoming events but are Here-Now.

To sleep. Verb in transit! Do you know when you are asleep? Awareness is such a frail thing that it cannot teach you how to be conscious of your own sleep. Equally I cannot rely on the evidence of my own eyes, for they might lie to me. And my memory can only recall snatches of the truths that I have heard or seen.

Two of my Shadows walk past me. They do not see me, for their eyes are closed to all but their own world. Like mine. Like, something of a similar nature. What is Nature? What is similar? What am I? If I am a What? They wandered on and I followed their steps in the dark. A figurative dark for the day sun shone bright and it was warm. As lovers do, they linked arms and remained perfectly still, except for their feet, which moved. Had to because the pavement was passing underneath them.

I didn't conceive them as women but that is what they turned out to be. Females. Mere birth machines to some. I could ask them nothing because I could not think of the questions. As a result I shall never know if they knew who they were.

The fog rolled over the moorland and blotted out the sun. One of those summer chills descended on the place, so I moved on quickly just to keep warm. Through the mist I could make out the dim shape of houses. Yellowed windows watched me as I passed by forcing me, by their very malevolence, to keep going. And there was a half eaten bus-stop, huddled against a post box to keep warm. What it had been before it was a post box I don't know. A pill box that ate too much? Anyway I found myself filling the street and bumping into me often; buying and selling articles I neither wanted to sell or buy. There was only one thing that wasn't me and that was Riley, but before I could speak he lost himself in the Cloud of Unknowing and I couldn't find him. A half-world where I am neither one thing nor another. This is the glorious aluminium palace of the imagination. Gold-plated to one eye; crude and pitted with years to the other.

Not in either view do I belong. Briefly I meet others pacing the poop-decks and bridges of their minds and asking tentative questions out of misplaced politeness.

'Hello. Doing all the business?' Some of them are pop singers. Are they called that because they are all fizz and come out of a bottle?

I nod and smile. They just pass on, forget that they ever asked the question or even that I exist. This must be so because the next second I meet them they ask it all over again. It has an inevitability that matches death. What a wild cloth they weave! But, oh how easily it falls apart. It is as insubstantial as a spider's web to all but the flies that get caught in it. Albeit the fact that I can feel the sticky texture of my own web and see, in a kind of perspective, the wounds of experience. I do not belong for the web is brittle in my hands and I can break it; whereas they cannot. Like Marley's chains, their webs are steel hawsers, strangling their individuality, killing; as surely as any Glass Mountain.

My path stretches out as far as I can think, which is a short cosmic distance. My conception is a narrow thing despite my effort to extrapolate. The Stars' Dust is in my eyes and though I care I cannot see what is beyond my immediate self. I cannot even see my own feet.

There are weeping sores on my mind that I doubt if even time will heal. I search for them and lick them clean. Still the savage you see. And I know I must get away. But how? And, where?

The verdant moorland does not welcome me, nor do its folk. Yet I do love them. With salt in my eyes I turn and look back at the houses I knew as a child, just after the war when joy, like sweets, was rationed. They were homes then and held me tight to their breasts. Now they reject me. Perhaps I have learned to fly and they no longer want me in the nest? A fledgling must learn to face the world and love it because of its faults, not in spite of them. When I try to speak No one puts words, his words, where mine should be; only then is No one satisfied with the answers, and cannot see that they have turned into questions, unanswerable.

But even knowing this does not help me find myself. I must look beyond that meagre depth.

Peep, peep, peep, back, backyard, full of dead loves and the frayed shirtails of ambitions. Renold, you're not even half human. RENOLD? RENOLD, DO YOU HEAR ME? The sound of my own screaming curtain lifts from my eyes and, for a second, I see the dingy room. Old and dingy. Is that the same as dingy and old? But there they are.

'Come now my Lord, surely thou dost not think that I will countenance thy action?'

'Buckingham, I care not whether ye countenance or no but We will have Essex on the block by noon or thou shalt take his place.'

Shades, oh Shades that once were mortal, why do you not die and let the world forget your crimes?

The actors removed their wigs and faces and answered me by throwing me into a butt of malmsey.

Tradition! Thus Spake Zarathustra: Topol too.

Predictable as yesterday's news.

That, 'still,' small voice has gone now. I feel a little better.

And I am dressed better these days. My Shadows like to be reminded of their past, it helps them face the future and anyway in the past they can always be on the winning side. Who said there ain't no 'ifs' in history?

Hey hey, along the path
down to the garden gate gyrating gravel.
Tousled head in frame of curls and laughter
See bright thing, pebble pick up and pocket
No thought of what comes after.
Little, little, little, thing,
to my bower poses bring.
I know you well, but do you know me?
Your eyes are blank, that I can see!
'Yes, Jester, I know you, but aren't you out your time?'
Ages, places, people, faces, runners races,
all the same,
timeless game.
So the Jester courts and pleases,
On whatever time his fancy seizes.

The Jester chuckles, not at the rhyme but at the antics. His eyebrows raised, he sings again.

It was for Renold that you called
Although your cry appalled, my sense
of rhythm and of rhyme,
I had to come from out of time.

His smile was that of a man believed to be an idiot but who knows he is far from that. This is because when all the others have been killed *he* will still be alive and kicking.

'Do you have to speak in rhyme?'

'No, it's a terrible bore really but it's expected of you. Same as everybody expects a fallen angel to be wicked! They're not as a rule you know. I mean all they had was a Marxist Style Revolution but committed the unforgivable crime of losing.'

'Have you ever met a fallen angel then?'

'Heh, heh, of course I have. I am a jester, in fact, the Jester. I'll have you know I've entertained Lucifer Himself.'

'You mean the Devil?'

'Is that what he's called now? Oh yes, I've played before him, and at the Command Performance before the Holy One.'

'You sort of commute between Heaven and Hell so to speak?'

'That's right my boy. My, you do catch on fast!'

'But isn't that rather difficult? I mean the two camps can't exactly be the best of friends.'

The Jester roars with laughter.

'Hey, that's good, you're a comedian did you know. I must use that some time. I could turn you into a jester inside, oooh a couple of centuries. Of course it isn't difficult to travel between the two places. They're both inside *you*; or me for that matter. But after the break-up of the empire, when His Magnificence saw that he couldn't ever regain complete control, He gave them their independence. Couple of centuries later things began to settle down and now well, His Magnificence and His Magnificence have a game of Cosmicology at the slightest excuse.'

'Why do you give them both the same title?'

'Dear, dear my boy. Didn't your mother ever tell you that when you *have* to work for two masters, you must treat them both the same or have your ectoplasm boiled?'

'But surely –'

'Shut up boy! They've ears like a Ganymedian Sand Flea!' He stood up and frightened me to death, 'well, I must be off now, bye bye.'

He didn't exactly vanish, so much as become pinpointed and I couldn't get the smell of sulphur out of my nostrils for years. When I turned to leave I tripped over a twisted dream he had left tangled round my hopes, and the galaxy laughed for a millennium.

I wish there was some kind of Tippex for the sheets of life, so that they could be rewritten somehow. As of writing I have had another stroke, a minor one, thank you Riley, and cannot speak clearly. My words stop somewhere between my brain and my mouth. Yet, if I take time, your time? I can type. Each letter taking think time longer than it, they ought. Decision was, do I put it in or not? The ages are going by and *I* can't run after them. Am I talking sense now, don't know but the fire inside says try. Debts must be paid and myne is a massv one. Each word has to be cleared, they are all there somewhere. Can you take, that is the wrong word, stand? Don't know. The effort, the minutes I think before each word. Is enough. Will rest.

Chapter Six

There is an out-of-focus television and a badly tuned-in radio constantly playing in my mind. I can keep on moving the aerial but still cannot get a clear picture or static free sound. But that does not mean I am unaffected by the sudden events of the cries and the dying of the hungry. Those hungry for food or for love.

I met a child walking by the soft pit of the grave. How surged the anger when I saw its head, bowed low in its quiet sorrow and yet, there was a cackle emerging from the effulgent halo round its head. Down the mossy embankment the grass stretched thirstily at the soil and river water; it was there the stone-filled path led. My Shadows were thick and fast here and the child stood and watched them, a slight smile on its impassioned face.

Not daring to speak, in case he called my name, I slipped past him and made my way through the rough crowds out on to the pier. Its planks were rotten and creaked beneath the weight of me and my chair. As I watched a greedy-gurgle popped its head out of the turgid river for an instant and lashed its tongue at me. I spat in its face and stepped quickly back, out of its way.

Which ever way I turn there's always Something waiting for me. You see that white shirttail of the water? It looks so innocent yet holds certain death. You can't breathe water, you know. I've tried it; all you get is a tickle in the throat and no oxygen. But that doesn't stop my lemmings of Shadows from taking their millennial dip. Fascinated I listened to the Drone.

'One, two, three ... four, five, six; come along now, move up quickly or we'll be behind schedule.' The Drone is forever counting but it ain't rosary beads.

They obeyed of course and quite naturally, that was their purpose in life. The Drone had a lot of sacks to fill. I knew if I stayed my turn would come, so I moved a minute away where I would be safe out of their time and, for that matter, the Drone's time. Someone asked me if I felt better. I could make her read the words which said that Better didn't want to be felt but preferred to keep her knickers on. On either side of Someone's head two lumps jumped up and down and then she went away.

From my vantage point on my Second's Hill I watched for a few hundred years and wished that No one hadn't cut the strings on my harp. I couldn't get into heaven without it. My music had been taken away because I had been naughty. The Catcher told me that. My Catholic taste had been burned at the stake as heresy. No one had hidden Bach, Grappelli, *West Side Story*, Gilbert and Sullivan and even my guitar. My fingers had sent a message to say that they were off on holiday and wouldn't be back. I tried to clear the jam but they wouldn't listen, wouldn't listen to my fractured words. One dark Someone kept muttering into the fog round his eyes. 'I hear what you're saying.' Renold translated for me.

'It's a bit like politicians. It means: I don't like you or what you are trying to say and have no intention of taking any bloody notice!'

When I looked I could see the Someone's ears were studded with prejudice and large notice that said, 'I've made up my mind and whatever you say isn't going to change it.' I sat, accused of Soul-Murder and, although innocent, no defence witness was called. And if they came unasked were told to bugger off.

Riley was sitting by the roadside, his rump on a mossy bank. Tears streamed down his face and his wares lay about him all broken and smashed. His tiny mongrel dog was twitching, sniffing at some of the more obscure sects, worrying them as he would a rat. I could see that my Shadows had grown tired of him and had tarred and feathered him. I did not speak because you have little of use to say to someone who has been tarred and feathered. But the jiggly-jangly-jumble of his gods was a sad thing to say. Poor Riley, he had meant no harm. Down the corridor I could see some No ones and a very few Someones sharpening mental nails; getting ready for a crucifixion.

I saw the sad polyp standing by the Stones, just outside the cell door. It had tooth bites in its neck and was chattering in fear by Castor's side. Which twin shall die by becoming immortal? Not the Counting Child, not the lemmings, not the Shadows, not I.

'Ooooooo! They were such good little gods,' muddy mumbling from the feather-sticky object weeping into the depths of his own confusion. 'Lao Tzu, Confusussed, or Confucius, Lao Tzued!'

From my minute away moment I realised that I could have escaped the Counting Child in some other way; but then, time-jumping is my natural bent so it follows I could use it. No sense in the equivalence that could have by-passed the cumulus Clouds of Unknowing. There was, it seemed no end, no chippings to be swept up and glued together to form some relevant philosophy. Their meanings had been torn up, destroyed, like love letters from someone the heart has forgotten. The dark Someone was muttering into his filing cabinet, the one where he kept his pet armadillos called ideas. 'I'm not here to help advise or help you solve your problems; problems; only you can do that' I am mystified. What is he here for then? When he turns round I can see his face sprinkled with 'I've decided dust'. So I go to the cemetery. It's quiet there and there's no one to threaten you. But there is a Magnificent Silence which I wish could be filled with music. But it has been taken from me away with colour. All shapes are dim by the pit's side. No dancing, no singing, no warmth, no thing, no peace. A seeming finality. And yet, in a distance I cannot single out as having definition or precision, there is a faint, faint sound.

A soft mewling of a clarinet, dribbling notes in a hesitant flow. A gentle tonguing of the instrument by one who loves. I cannot tell whether it is classical or jazz which does not matter, for it is the sound itself which does.

In the cellar-dark of his intent I strain to hear his sound creation; mute, for while I hear, my heart rests. Here is the voice of the Soul that would otherwise be dumb. He sees me across the room-filled smoke but does not stop playing and I do not wish him to, my Perennial Pan breathing his pyretic, soothing the pain.

His eyes close and the Shadows fluctuate like faulty neons; becoming clear and then fading back to their natural grey. He is a person!

This chapter on this miasmic saga is difficult to write because the *Now* me is not clear-eyed and fluffy-tailed. That makes it more difficult to watch the puppet's play on Time's backcloth a problem to read. You will have seen a small bulb warming, but at the moment the flimmerty, fragile lace of the picture is still a half-tone, grey-red, black yellow, gold with a rough, smooth atmosphere loaded with doubt. Mazy smoke, mingling with the Shadows, make it difficult to tell Shadow from smoke. The criss-cross meaningless talk heating up the atmosphere with wild senseless argument. Its harsh whisper in conflict with the sense-tingling sound of the musician.

But I am still separated from the sound and wonder if my Shadows can think. Do they think of not destroying the magic with their ceaseless chatter? They don't have want to have to give up their endless convulsions. The split aeon of torment passes and for an instant I can bathe in the silk-soft sea he is weaving. I want to drown in his music, drain every last drop of emotion from his playing and know I'm in deep. Yet the thin thread of consciousness tethers me securely and I cannot break free of my Shadows and their effects.

Who shall say *no* to this? Dare I say it? Here where the brown earth and the Counting Child wait. There is no calculable millennium, no finite goal, nothing that can be measured; except the tread of Someone's feet in yesterday's corridor on the cat's paw carpet. Unquestionable fear lurks behind the Shadows as they dream of immortality. I am so tired of the wild whimsy and No one's cold conjecture. They are hurtling along in a body-clash so narrow in their passing, they almost become nothing and the property of the Counting Child; their minds oblivious to terror.

Terror! What is this thing? Is it a thing? A frayed shirt cuff before an interview with fiscal suicide at the bank. It creaks through the night in the haggard hours before the horror of the day. Where mud-bubbles bleed a halitosis of bad ideas that stink like cabbage water left for weeks in a sink of pale placebos, *usque ad nauseam*, and the screaming of a child crushed beneath a lorry's wheels; longing for a death that will not come. Terror *in situ*, fermenting evilly. No one doesn't understand the terror and I wonder if it can be diluted with familiarity, like contempt. I must ask Riley if he ever manages to get the tar off.

Do they keep bottles of it, stored like wine in racks, and keep it to see if it improves with age? All I know is what I feel and how I am trapped. But just think, how would it be if you could buy a bottle or handful of terror for a few quid.

I must climb out of this well into the sunlight however weak it is. When I do, I find the town is empty, which is not altogether surprising. The packet of dream-sticks in my pocket ache to be used. But they are a poor palliative with which to soothe the weeping nerve ends of my brain and isolation.

Dear friend, this has, to date, been by far the hardest to compose. However I think its pain is apparent and therefore needs no other validation that what is here set down. No, I was far from well when it was being typed; to me, that makes it all the more important. Of course, I am feeling a great deal better now but whether I shall tomorrow also is another matter. Such is the nature of the beast and always was. I never knew/know when the world was/is going to slip from my fingers. Physically things improved with the help of my physio-terrorists. The girls know I don't mean that and so should you. By now it is such a feeble joke, I sort of wonder that I dare make it.

You know there is talk about healing hands? Well, that is what my physios possessed, I am sure and refuse to be convinced otherwise. They also have endless care and patience. Okay girls stop blushing, I shall probably be rude to you in a minute and say something like, 'Why are your hands always so bloody cold?' You do it on purpose I am sure, just to see us squirm. There! Is that more in character?

I must ask you to keep in mind that I am trying to recreate for you, what I saw, thought and felt. This is aided by today's confusions, doubts and pensive wanderings, when I *still* cannot find the words I need without a search that borders on desperation. When meanings are gone from the most ordinary things, so the kettle becomes, 'that metal thing for putting liquid in'. When I don't *see* things straight and/or it takes minutes to say, 'yes', to a question. When some would say I am hallucinating. Actually, I'm never closer than the edge of that. For even when having a TIA, unless I lose consciousness, I always retain a spark, a glimmer, a something of the real. That is why this can have no strict chronology; that the clock's hands have not stopped turning and rested at a given point is of no moment. This is no *Marie Celeste* with the hot food still on the table but not a soul behind. The hot food *is there* but we, we are in the here/now as well as in the *then*. You know, when in a lift or on a rollercoaster, we speak of leaving our stomachs behind? Well, we've sort of stayed where we are, and, at the same time gone back to see where I left my mind. As if it were a handbag or something.

Several people had a go at picking it up but they weren't too successful; mostly because they were looking in the wrong place or couldn't find the right handles. And, has been explained, I have been given an all too sharp reminder that what happened in the past, can happen again, despite medication.

Nevertheless some picture postcards do stick out as I've said. Impinged themselves on the shaky edifice of my consciousness. One such is thus.

You know the six-bed bays one is put in, when not so ill as to require a single room. Well, there one has temporary friends. I could not speak, read or write and across from me was the obligatory ward comic. The usual kind-hearted type who, despite a serious heart condition, knowing I could not move, was for ever getting out of bed for newspapers (not for me of course), sweets and so on for all the others in the bay. And, naturally, he was full of jokes. For me he was helpful in that he filled in my menu card for me. He read out what was on offer and I indicated which I preferred or disliked least. He also, shush, kept nipping off for a forbidden fag.

One day, during kit-inspection when Zeus and his officers came round asking things like, 'He still alive?' Surprise being palpable. Why Zeus should be surprised is a mystery. Has he no faith in his panoply of terrified angels and archangels? He leant across me for a full thirty seconds, told me to try and hold his fingers with my right hand and asked how I was feeling. Silly bugger, he knew I couldn't speak. Then he gets to the comic and thunders, even the walls quake.

'You, Mr —, I shall refuse to treat,' there are traces of steam coming out of his ears as he almost bellows, '*you* are still smoking. Anyone who smokes deserves to get sick!'

The small ward is still with shock and his entourage electric with embarrassed unease. The comic is unmoved. He smiles beatifically and, from under his bedclothes, produces an oblong parcel.

'I know it's your birthday soon, Doctor, so I've brought you a present. Do open it.'

Zeus is nonplussed and, it has to be admitted, charmed. He accepts the gift and unwraps it. There are a variety of sharp breath intakes. Two angels turn and walk hurriedly away, stethoscopes stuffed into mouths. Zeus is speechless. Well, what can you say to a box of twenty of your favourite cigars?

Chapter Seven

You can see, you can hear, but cannot respond in what is even remotely called a 'normal', way. Everywhere is empty, there's no one, nothing but a saturated singularity of 'aloneness'. You cannot reach out to anything by either word or deed. All you can feel is your Self, sinking through this black pool of waiting/hoping that what people tell is true and that there really is a 'Sun', out there somewhere. That those, the waiting/hoping are the stillborn twins of an everlasting Terror Thrawn Winter. What matters is that which is Real. That which is Real matters. That seems to make some sort of sense but there is a catch of course; what do you mean by Real? Betwitchment by words. That is what Professor Emmet says, and by words, shape, sound and meaning I was persistently bewitched. But then, most of us are all the time as philosophers keep telling us. No wonder they are not the most popular of people.

Even meeting, 'friends' – I use the term loosely to describe anyone who doesn't cringe with embarrassment whenever you put in an appearance – can be a problem. You can never be absolutely sure whether a person is a friend, or not. Whether they are going to accept you for what you are or whether they're going to make some kind of judgement about you. All too often you discover the person you regarded as a friend turns out not to be. That when you are not with them they have made unkind remarks about you, your clumsiness, your speech or some other aspect of your behaviour that is slightly out of kilter with what they regard as polite and correct. And such back-stabbing is not, I'm afraid, confined only to those ignorant of the illness. Professionals, who should know better, can be just as guilty. Several friends – I mean it this time – who, like me, have had strokes tell of singularly unsympathetic unhelpful social workers. One actually went so far as to describe her social worker as, 'that woman, my enemy'. This is not just a sad state of affairs, it is disastrous. If it is felt that you need a psychiatric social worker then that person should be utterly trustworthy and, in my opinion, as reliable as the Confessional. This is because the sufferer is absolutely vulnerable, without defence, physically, emotionally and, in some cases, mentally. The professionals should know that such is the state of mind that any criticism, however mild, can be and nearly always is, a crushing blow to an ego already hurting, wrecked or damaged, perhaps beyond repair. How often do you see people with some kind of brain damage or who have had strokes, just shoved into a corner and left. If spoken to at all, shouted at. As if they were deaf and stupid, not bewildered, wounded and hurting inside deep inside; wanting to get out but unable to without help. What people like this are doing is throwing a concrete belt to a drowning man.

I have a sort of memory of being in a café. My wife had taken me in and bought me a coffee, or I may have bought it myself, I can't remember. Just across the room were two people. Clearly they knew me but I did not know them as such. I mean, I may have known them but even now cannot recall either their names or faces. The only thing I do know is that they were discussing me and not to my advantage. The only reason I know this is that the waitress, a real friend, told me and said I was not to worry, they were just daft and didn't know any better. The problem is that because I still don't know who they were or what they were saying. I wake up at night worrying about it even now. That incident and others like it nag at you persistently, I mean the above happened about six years ago I think. I wonder if they know how much hurt they caused and are still causing? By the grace of God I have been incredibly lucky and made a sort of recovery and am, to some extent, able to rationalise about it and feel some kind of pity for them in the sense that they hadn't got anything better to think or talk about. Sorry folks, time to dive in again but don't hold your breath. Inhale deeply that beautiful, polluted by diesel fumes, air.

From the deep of that well, I try to climb out into the weak sunlight like I said. The town was empty, which again, as I said, doesn't surprise me as it always was; and there is an oppressive venom of isolation. Bright lights flash rhythmically, heart-counting and relays click like unseen insects. Dancing currents of Alpha and Omega came and went, went and came. I watch the pattern evolving but it never moved or became moving. Soulless, unintelligent, lifeless almost. I am surprised that it couldn't at least leave with the spirit it came with.

Intangibles, essences, abstracts, that my Shadows are always making mechanical grabs at. Naturally they never succeed in catching anything for it is Crudity, wild and without restraint. The Praetorian Guard sold an empire and the purchaser found he had brought a speedy demise, an expensive suicide. Might as well try to cut smoke or balance an elephant on an egg.

Which brings me to Eggheads. As a race they are a curious folk, in both senses. Always searching for scientific truths or ephemeral ones, but mostly only finding questions. Too often their premise is all set out before they make the search. Which means they can't see the Truth when they see it. I wonder why they're called Eggheads? I cracked one open once, an egg I mean; it was all runny with a glob of yellow stuff in the middle. It had a high viscosity though; that means it was thick. Anyway you never find anything you are looking for until you stop looking. Of course, all that proves is that you've passed from the dimension where you left it, to one where it isn't; so of course you can't find it. Perhaps that's what I've done to/with my mind. Look over there, they're having a party.

Crêpe paper and kunzle cakes decorate the table and some of absolutely anything; you'll get my Shadows all of a dither and then you know what will happen:

> Half a ton of nuclear juice
> Half a ton of uranium.
> Mix it up and make it nice,
> Bang goes a nation.

'*Et cum spiritu tuo.*'

'Shut up you old fool.'

'I beg your pardon, my son?'

'I'm not your son!'

'In the eyes of God you are.'

'Maybe, but which God and how do I know He's looking at me?'

'Heh, heh! Precisely, marvellous isn't it?'

'I don't follow you.'

'Neither does anyone else!'

'Now look here priest – '

'I don't want to, you're not a pleasant sight/site!'

'Who the Hell d'you think you are?'

'Certainly not Hell, otherwise nobody in particular.'

'You're trying to confuse me.'

'No I'm not.'

'YES YOU BLOODY ARE!%' (The percentage sign is necessary to indicate the degree of frustration.)

Breathe deeply, force control, raise the eyes skyward, well, look at the ceiling from where I'm lying on the carpet. I think it's the carpet. It's hard and scratchy anyway. The priest? Sends echoes round the room.

'My occupation in life, well this life, is to make things clearer.'

'What things?'

'All sorts of things.'

'Liquorice all sorts?'

'Don't be impertinent!'

'Now, now, priesty, temper temper!'

'Get thee behind me, Satan.'

Disappearing act number two, section four, paragraph six, Devil's Manual Phwwwtttttt!

'Where are you?'

'Behind you, where you told me to go!'

'AAARRRGHGHRrararahghghg!'

What an odd fellow for a priest! I thought we were getting on quite well. I must say though, that was a beautiful puff of blue smoke he disappeared in. People are so disappointing.

It must be something to with animated magnetism. I mean I cannot think of any other reason for my Shadows to cluster round me? It's very misleading because it took me years to find out I wasn't the centre of the universe. Next time I'm in Moscow, I'll have a word with Lenin about it. He wasn't the centre either but for a while thought he was. Then he went and spoilt the whole effect by dying. Must have quite upset him. Shaw had words to say on that question while having a chat with Methuselah.

I sat there stirring my tea until it got cold and then I drank it. That's because I was thinking and that can be dangerous. Jesus was crucified, Socrates poisoned, in fact most of our thinkers are got rid of one way or another. Hounded to death because they had something important to say. Problem is I can't say anything. Perhaps that's good for my health. There should be a government health warning on talk. I just blew a smoke ring. Rather surprising because I'm not smoking, at least not where it shows. Sorry. I will write out a thousand times in Sanskrit, 'I must not make sexual allusions.' Oh, what a beautiful little black triangle of fuzz. Twin Peaks here we come. How the white river floweth.

'You're at it again aren't you?'

'You're never alone with a Conscience. Blast it!'

'Now, now, where would you be without me?'

'Happy!'

'Don't be cynical. It doesn't suit you.'

'I'm not a cynic. One of those is a failed idealist,' but I sigh in a kind of acknowledgement of defeat.

'That's better. Be a good boy.'

'You going to leave me alone now?'

'I might if you behave yourself. In fact I nearly intervened when you were talking to that priest, but I felt that you had a point.'

'Yeah. Well you're intervening now, so belt up!'

'All right, all right,' pause, 'do you remember the good times we had when we were a child?'

'Naturally. The bad ones tend to get forgotten.'

'You realise I had a fairly easy job then?'

'Could have now it you weren't so fond of sticking your nose into our affairs.'

'That is a bloody silly remark. You know we can't avoid each other. Inextricably bound together, that's us.'

'Yeah. Don't I know it!'

LAUGHTER HIGH-PITCHED AND UNCONTROLLED.

'You see that fellow over there, the one with the wart on his curiosity?'

'Yes, what about it?'

'Well, he keeps looking at us, me that is, as if I'm crazy.'

'Yes, and there'll be little men in white coats chasing you if you don't start behaving.'

'There'll be little green ones if I don't stop drinking this stuff.'

'Perhaps fear will work where Reason can't or won't. I wish Plato would put the horses back between the shafts; the chariot won't go far without them.'

'Boooooo!'

'Now isn't that strange. It frightened my conscience and not me?'

A purple raincoat just walked passed the window smoking a cigarette. The blinds had been drawn across the sky and it was dark. Ergo, he, whatever it was, was walking in the raincoat, er, window, sky? I'll get it right if it kills me, DARK.

I want to catch a bus and go from London to Manchester. It won't serve any purpose but at least I'll see a bit of the countryside. Could try a bit of gun-running if I could find one that could. They ought to be able to, I mean they're always running out of bullets, except in cowboy films. No, better not, just stand on the touchline and encourage your favourite team instead. One of them is bound to win but its painful on the crotch, fence-sitting. That's why some politicians are the shape they are and long to get into the House of Pee-ers. I wonder if I shall live long enough to grow old? It doesn't seem likely; it's just that I'm not keen on long journeys.

Happy meeting! Two young animals preparing to mate. Hands clasped in a transient joy, eyes dream-blessed and lips eager; so very eager.

Be still my children, be still, live your love and love your living but remember, my everlasting darlings, above all else be friends, real friends. Because if you aren't, what are you going to do for the other twenty-three hours of the day? And what will you do when terror strikes at the roots of lives? Promises can break the heart as well as mend it and, of the two, love is the oak, friendship the willow. Storms can break an oak where the willow bends but does not snap. Love is when the other person's happiness is essential to your own; knowing that you can never possess them or even want to try.

Chapter Eight

Exspectans exspectavi Dominum et repexit me; et exaudivit depreca-tionem meam. Psalm 40.

And on some rain-dead days we were taken out into the town – where market stalls, gaily-green, orange, lime and red fruit lies profusionwise. Canopy of time and weather-chewed canvas stretched taut, yet somehow remaining limp and disreputable, shields the underneath from desultory daylight. It's there to keep the rain off. Sole-wet cobbles, slippery with spoiled celery, mingle with cardboard boxes and legs. Plastic carrier bags wander about in single-minded confusion. Where, what and how to buy? Cash, forced to go further than it should, cries like a tired child. Grapes huddle together in an effort to avoid acid-hungry eyes The air has a brittle taste.

My Shadows get their sustenance here. They get their cauli-flowers, pease and avocado pears. This is where they feed their bodies while their minds are dying of starvation. Their animated puppetry makes me laugh as they barter for a ragged cabbage as if it were a Rembrandt. In a way it is a work of art more complete than any painting, but then oil and canvas would not be very palatable. Sorry about that.

They were intent on what they were doing and through the mist I could just about detect the faint glow of conscious effort. But all their efforts went to serve the Kublai Khans of this world and the only things they want are frequent pats on their pockets. Are they happy in their fiscal harems? Surely even a lust like that should be satiated by success? It turns from the chrysalis of cash into the Death's Head Moth of power.

A temporary insanity that's what. Then there's no fear of even a minor retribution. A mild case, vague and tenuous, no harm can come to them for all their machinations are diffused by figures moving on a tiny screen.

'Come and buy, come and buy!'

'What?'

'I don't know but you might as well buy it anyway. Take it on faith.'

'How can buy it if I don't know what, it is?'

'Stop being awkward!'

'Ah, well there you have it. I like being awkward.' Thinks, at least that's what you think; can't see beyond your own irritation to the suppurating boil of pain I carry around with me.

The barker gave me a withering look and a pineapple. Neither of them were very good, the look wouldn't have withered the skin off a dead rice pudding and the pineapple was sour.

What a load of rot it all is. Better go back to barter. At least that was logical and there were no adverts. Not to say that they didn't have their worries.

'Hey you! Wake up at the back there or I'll have you fined for wasting your father's cows.'

The Haunted Fishtank in the corner of the room is talking.

'Here is the news. The government is to pay four million pigs, twenty million loaves and one fish for the new American fighter. Taxi drivers are to get a rise of one rabbit a week, skinned.' There's no end to the variations. Just think of your bank statement. No Hubert it is not ludicrous, cretinous maybe, but not ludicrous. You just *try* to adjust to an outside world that doesn't make *any* kind of sense.

Someone or something just spoke to me. I'm not sure which. They didn't say anything, just mouthed a few words. Fruitstall philosophy as perennial as Huxley's and probably just as relevant in many ways.

The stockmarket opened early and jangled its chains at me. Several people had made a killing the day before apparently but not one of them was imprisoned. And the Leading Bowler Hats marched in a meaningless procession round the ground of London. Don't tell anyone, but it's actually a magical ritual, where all the best tips are exchanged in the toilet. That brought a flush to the cheeks of the recipients. But moves could not be made until they had returned to the floor and only then if there was no cry of, 'Fourteen Hundred,' to break the spell.

I watched them at their play in a moment of blind, penetrating sadness. Their Golden Rules, thoughts and romances chained to a fixed span. Why can't they see that they are trying to drink from an empty bottle. They gave us pennies to spend. Little round flat things that smelt of fading greed. They wanted me to know what to do with them. The coins I mean, but I didn't want any polo mints, I don't like the taste of the hole in the middle.

'Money is necessary,' said the beetle-browed banker, holding up his rolled umbrella with the ballpoint spike for ticking off the minutes of my life. He pats his paunch and looks expensive. I ask him if he's got an ulcer and he tells me off for being personal and threatens to call a policeman.

'You can't.'

'Why not?' he demands.

'Because this is my dream not yours!' I retort. This frightens him so much he turns into a filing cabinet labelled 'Credit Restrictions', and won't come out. He grinned.

'Don't worry, he always does that when some one frightens him. It's all due to the fact that the Vietnam War cost him all his pocket money.' He pats my shoulder and says,

'Leave him to me. It'll be all right you'll see; come and help me paint the Sistine Chapel.'

How can they call lying flat on your back, paint dripping down your arms, rehabilitation? I have puzzled many times just who the He is I am referring to and for the life of me I just do not know. The best I can come up with is that He was an occupational therapist. All of them talk to you about day-to-day events while trying to get you perform given tasks. I think it helps.

Where was I in this last section? I can't be absolutely certain but am pretty sure it is a mixture of a hospital shop, the office where our pocket money was doled out, pension books having been taken in, and an organised trip somewhere.

Chapter Nine

I knew I had to find some kind of pattern for survival. It might lie in watching the dancers on the green outside the church. But not, I was certain of this, on a couch in a quiet room where a man muttered softly to himself, making marks on paper after watching me fumble with some brick-like things. At least I think they were bricks.

From somewhere there is the sound of a tired bell set in a squat tower built of stone for an imagined posterity. But I cannot respond to its call. I am too tired and confused. My mind's hands are sore with heaving at rope hawsers in capstan-twisted man hours. The bright days are few and sun-spilled hours fewer.

I see, I hear but I do not conquer. The rage and frustration is as trapped as I. No one cannot see the effect of my effort. At least it seems that way to me.

Why do my Shadows need toys? A child needs them in order learn. Is it that my Shadows are children? My Shadows fluctuate like damaged light bulbs and are affected by the weather which produces all kinds of variants to the attitude and poses they strike in the ceiling in the eking out of their fractured lives.

Today it is wet, yesterday it was cold, tomorrow, well who knows if some one will be able to solve this crossroad. My extremities are always cold, the nails, tiny and pink.

I hear a red-throated cry, shredding the air with a razor blade. Fear bespoken by a vicious tailor. And I have a poet's albatross round my neck, caught by his net of words. It is remembered knowledge only, long gone; its pages scattered to the wind-drifted sea. Round and round it goes in tight in scream-frightened circles. But this is no Banshee. It is, I discover, me. I want to go home. Mummy can't be far away. I'll wait at this bus-stop.

In the crushed world a Softly-Voice tries to heft the pain from me.

'Mum's dead darling.'

'Dead?' I am soaked to the skin, the road gravelled under slippered feet. Who killed her?

The Softly-Voice caresses my hand and tells me Age killed her. What right had He got to kill my mother? I demand a recount: that election must have been rigged. She isn't dead. I can still see her, there at the bed-end, smiling and Torquay happy in the sand. The Softly-Voice is weeping quietly in the sharpened dark, and me? I am angry. Why did no one tell me that mother had to go away on that business trip? They never tell me anything. I hate the Chamber of Commerce. That rings hard and loud with sirens and the dogs of war. Each night I go collecting bus-stops 'coz that's where mummy is. And the Chamber. No silly, not the one that lives under the bed; mind, it's just as full of effluence. But I must get to the bus-stop! The Softly-Voice presses me back, her tears as wet as mine. She has been hurt and I have an urge to kill whoever did it. Hate is long-lived but Love, that is immortal.

Someone joins the Softly-Voice and folds a ragged cloth I recognise as Grief and puts in a box atop the wardrobe. I long for sanctuary and for the matters that are real. For what is real matters. But how to understand? I am deaf-blind to understanding, and nearly drown in the word collisions flying like ships before the wind.

Why do you bounce on the bed? I know you made it and therefore, can do with it what you like, but you are not the only inhabitant. Others had a hand in its creation, you burbling great goon! They say that dripping water can wear away a stone. Well,

I am the drip and life is the stone. That's what's wrong, the blueprint never works out in practice. I am so weary. So tired of trying. Will the spring never come? I feel like taking a bath, in sulphuric acid. But the Softly-Voice and Someone urge me to drink from the bitter cup. They want me to believe in Santa Claus and the Tooth Fairy. Well, why not? Can't be any worse than Riley. Three steps forward and two back. A macabre waltz but the snail can get out of the well. They say lightening never strikes twice in the same place. Well, I can tell you it does. It had three goes at me and threw in a hell of a lot of small power cuts just for good measure.

There was a fare of taxis hunched together in their beds by the cathedral. From time to time, according to some unspoken rule, they dash off to pick up a Shadow and carry him to paradise or some other theme park. I was in one once, but I did not like not being in control. Most of the time though they just sit in the sun contemplating their drain plugs. I wanted to go into the cathedral but was frightened there might be Someone there with pockets full of pills and needles. I'd eaten plenty of those and didn't like their taste any more. I mean you can have too much of a good thing. But even from the outside I can smell the incense and Someone's hand on my shoulder suggests that the tiny dot I've just spotted isn't an embryonic leopard, but a candle and that I am the moth which must fly towards it, even at the risk of being burned. And I did, I am sure, catch a glimpse of a rose the other day before the greenfly ate it. It's no use muttering about injustice when *you're* the judge of everything around you. But there were spiders' webs of thought, sticky, but fragile, reaching out, trying to catch the sounds and pictures around me and make them stay still enough, long enough for me to make sense of them.

I café sat-sipping-coffee and trying to remember when I had last seen BR. I knew I should know him but large as he was, he was insubstantial and hazy. Had he been a Shadow? Probably.

But his friendliness was touching my very being like nothing had for a long, long time. It was like discussing a character from a novel or play. My mind turned the information over and over until it had almost made a duvet out of it. I was bewitched by words, sounds, tastes, colours and textures. They had to be unmixed. How could you turn an omelette back into an egg? At least there had been no pity in BR's eyes. He had just been BR and that was something I *had* to hang on to. Then there was a blinding face-slapping flash. BR's wife had died. Was this a re-awakening or would fate, impersonal and without malice, smack me in the face again?

Let's not try to follow any rules but apply to the Department of Rule Dodging and book a regular supply of Dodges. That way I could fool myself into doing what my Self really wanted to do; i.e., get on with my life. I had a word with the man in the office and asked if he'd put in a requisition for some new dodges. He was quite indignant and told me that they even wanted him to clock-in in the mornings. It was all part of a rationalisation plan. But after a few words with his Secretary we decided on a plan to keep the sky's tears off. I could cover my confusion with a plastic mac. One constructed from inverted opinions of myself and, by working backwards, was able to go forward. But even going forward can have its problems.

For example how do you explain to the carpet that you would much stand or sit on it, rather than lie on it having fallen over? How do you explain the same thing to the person or persons who find you there? Convince them that you are not indulging in some kind of esoteric Yoga? I suppose you could be having a party with the House Dust Mites, always assuming your eyes are good enough to see them and they don't mind you dropping in. But anyway there you are, lying there wondering if you've broken something. Obviously you would know if you've damaged your good side but with your bad one there's no way of knowing. And it can happen so quickly. A step forward, that's what it is, or was meant to be. My beloved always claims it's my sneaky way of getting out of doing the washing up.

She had just nipped up to the garage to get something, I can't remember what and it doesn't matter. I decided that I'd show her how well I was getting on by doing the washing up whilst she was out. So I went through to the kitchen, hauled myself upright by the edge of the sink but forgot the brakes on my wheelchair. Sod's Law came into play, I went more dizzy than usual, fell, missed the chair completely as it shot backwards and hit the floor. The next thing I remember is Gwenllian and Christopher helping me up and into my chair, thence to my room. When she returned I was lying, like a beached whale half on, half off, the bed. I was too heavy for the children to lift as such. She straightened me out and rang for the doctor who came as usual and while he was examining me there was a wonderful crunch as my right shoulder went back into place having been dislocated. I didn't feel a thing, of course, because it was my right side. That was the good bit. The worst bit was that he insisted I went into hospital. I was there for a couple of days. Necessary of course but, while I am not phobic about hospitals which is a good thing, I have been rather too good a customer of theirs in the last eight to ten years.

Chapter Ten

Unlike *Gone with the Wind*, this cannot be a long book although it does have similarities with the title if not the text. I had felt like a lonely old man sitting in the middle of his years, counting his toes and wondering where all the joy had gone. I had climbed down from the hill and *gaped* at the gap where I had been. It was like steam on a window. You can draw pictures in it and then, with one quick swipe, whooosh! It's all gone. Everything was suspect, myself in particular. What *had* I done for God's sake. The Softly-Voice and Someones said 'nothing' but I found that difficult to accept and guilt gobbled at my vitals.

I had to wait and waiting is a very difficult thing to do. We are all, now, things. Patience is a quiet child but very, very persistent. I had to creep out of my own mediocrity and acknowledge what *could* be done, and then, go ahead and do it.

We have reached the ragged end of a *A Century of Echoes*, and like Blake, 'whatever I imagined I also saw'. And now to somehow meld the Daymare with the Real and make it a coherent whole. But you and I have something in common, because I am certain that at sometime in your life, you have been asleep; knowing that you are having a dream you do not like and trying desperately hard to wake up.

I, of course, was not asleep and could be talked at. Have you ever tried to take advice? He's an odd bloke, doesn't like to be taken anywhere; not funfairs, pubs, working breakfasts or Women's Institutes. He's particularly difficult when one of you is convinced another part of you doesn't exist. And he must be pretty big because there never seems a shortage of him to go round. Friends give him, professionals give him and even total strangers give him. You'll have noticed that I used the word, 'friends', that is because I was just beginning to realise that I had some. Had always had them but had to relearn the art of contact. Of course, there were the physical problems as well. They to a large extent remain but I don't bother about them any more. But for a moment try to imagine that you have a fifty-pound weight attached to your leg and something similar to your arm. Then imagine that all your fingers have a kind of impact adhesive and powerful spring attached to each joint. You will soon realise that trying to walk is an exhausting process and kicking the cat impossible. If a cup or something is put into your hand, it sticks to you like a limpet – you *cannot* let go of it. It's worse than getting bubblegum in your hair. You will readily see that a level of masochism is required to make any improvement.

It was like Columbus discovering the New World. It wasn't quite the one he was looking for, but it would do very nicely thank you, after all those months at sea. Okay, so there were a few nasties hiding in odd corners, but on the whole, life is pretty damn good. I will not dwell on Owen's death, except to say that it was a Cusp, and I owe him and my family a debt that will be paid whether they want me to or not.

I said at the beginning that perhaps it was the woodsmoke that brought it all back. Owen liked wood fires and cooking on them, you see. Thus you will see it was a cue, triggering something that enabled me, no, galvanised me, into real action. In the course of rehabilitation there were many such cues. Few led to complete memories and, as you would expect, it is still happening. Learning to read and write again was a painstaking process and one, I freely admit, had it not been for Owen's bullying, would have taken much, much longer. My speech therapist's report stated how willing and motivated I was. Hah! If only she'd known how I really felt; the yawning Chasm of self-doubt and frank disbelief it *could* be done. I genuinely thought it wouldn't. However, the fear of never reading again paled into insignificance when it became manifestly clear that somehow that third stroke, by far the worst, had delivered me from delusion. A rose was quite simply a rose once more. An ice-cream, an ice-cream. A kiss, a kiss. And, joy of joys, they gave me a wheelchair! That may seem odd to you but for years I had been unable to walk for more than a few steps and had fallen on numerous occasions, breaking ribs twice. But even had I been able to get around I wouldn't have known where I was, such was the distortion. My wheelchair has given me freedom. My mind is clear, except when I have a TIA and Julia and I can cope with those, because we now know what the sudden change in me actually is. We didn't before and not knowing, as anyone who has been ill will tell you, is many times worse than the illness itself. For your loved ones just as much as you. If I have a TIA now, I am just helped into bed by whoever happens to be around and there's always someone, I cannot be left alone, ever. But the children are quite matter-of-fact about it. I always thought it was Aunty Gladys that had funny turns. I don't think I've changed sex. The children I mean are Gwenllian and Christopher. She was four and he was two when I first became ill and therefore feel I have missed out on a large part of their childhood. But there is no point in grumbling about it, just get on and make up for lost time. So, if I can't kick the cat, I can always run over its tail, which is a lot more fun.

I have tried to show you exactly what it was like. I hope I have succeeded and that you will look at anyone who has suffered brain damage, for whatever reason, with new eyes. That you will understand we cannot see, hear, taste or touch things as you do and that very likely, inside, the real person is imprisoned.

Quite recently I was invited to be one of the audience and guests on the Anglia Television programme, *The Time, the Place.*

It was during Stroke Awareness Week and the programme had decided to centre on strokes among younger people. I had written to them in August 95 suggesting such a programme, but do not know whether that is why they actually did it. They did it very well I might say and all of us had a great time. However, I was in for a shock. I had thought that at forty-five, I had been young, but on that show and before it in the hotel and where we all met, back-stage, I met youngsters in their twenties. For me the really interesting point was that they all told identical stories to my own. They had met the same prejudices, lack of understanding and lack of acceptance. The same depressions, confusions and doubts and several, in private admitted that because they were so young to get what is perceived as a disease of the elderly, they had contemplated suicide; but of course commonsense had prevailed and they had fought back. Of course, there were times when *I* felt like saying, 'Goodbye Beloved World,' but never actually got round to it. That was because I was encapsulated by love, and deep down inside, knew it.

Where do we go from here? Upwards of course. I have it on good authority that Saint Peter has recently installed ramps for wheelchair users.

It has to be said that among the first things I began to find even remotely interesting, occupational therapy aside, was radio and in particular Radio Two, Radio Wales, and HTV. I have already made my thanks to them privately but take this opportunity to a public thank you to all Radio presenters. Why it should be that disembodied voices from a radio could manage to make contact with me, when those physically close couldn't, I haven't the faintest idea. I do know that I came to regard each one as a friend. They were/are always there you see, and it was to those presenters that I made my first tentative excursions back into the outside world. This by writing to them, to people like Terry Wogan or Derek and Ellen Jameson. There was an odd kind of safety in doing this. You will understand I was terrified of any outside contact. My physiotherapists might find that difficult to believe and the only answer I can give them is that the humour I displayed was my defence. A defence against a deep-seated fear of even being outside my bedroom. Instinct tells me that they probably did know I was scared to hell and dealt with me accordingly. But you will see why I could form a relationship with radio and, later, television personalities. They were in my home, my room, but represented no threat. I did not have to try and be sociable, in the accepted sense. I am absolutely certain there will be many who will instantly relate to this.

Of course re-forming normal (whatever that means?) relationships was very difficult. I think, from all that has preceded, this will have been made very clear; the lack of confidence I mean. Oh, sure you can put on a show for outsiders, and that includes doctors, therapists and the man from the Pru. So of course if anyone asks you if you're all right, assuming that you have understood the question, you automatically say, 'yes, fine,' when in reality you feel as if the roof has just caved in.

I have said to friends and have written about the fact that the last stroke changed me. But if you will bear with the reiteration, it felt as if a boil had burst. What had been twisted was now straight.

I hope I have given carers, professional and private, some insights into the damaged mind/brain. Also that I have given fellow sufferers Hope. Now we go forward, my family and I. There's a lot living I want to do and stories I want to tell. Thank you, all of you who treated and cared for me; especially as there must have been many times when you felt like giving up, that you had done all that could be done. And a special thanks to the Stroke Association; we couldn't have managed without you.

Come on lads and lasses, let's have fun! There's a great big beautiful world out there!